Navigating the Human Side of Boardroom Interactions

Navigating the Human Side of Boardroom Interactions

Improving Relationships at the Top

Thomas Sieber

BUSINESS EXPERT PRESS

Leader in applied, concise business books

First published in 2022 by
Business Expert Press, LLC
222 East 46th Street, New York, NY 10017
www.businessexpertpress.com

ISBN-13: 978-1-63742-291-5 (hardback)
ISBN-13: 978-1-63742-217-5 (paperback)
ISBN-13: 978-1-63742-218-2 (e-book)

Business Expert Press Corporate Governance Collection

First edition: 2022

10 9 8 7 6 5 4 3 2 1

Testimonials

"Thomas Sieber's book is a must-read on how to humanize the board room with an innovative perspective on board dynamics, social cohesion and challenger mindset if you want to go from old-school to new school board governance."—**Malou Aamund, Managing Director Google Denmark, Chairperson Thinkproject and board member DSV, KIRKBI, WSA, and LEGO Foundation.**

"Many boards have a set of incredibly successful individuals serving as directors. Yet as a team, they often 'play not to lose' instead of 'playing to win.' Thomas Sieber's excellent guide in understanding the 'human side of board interactions' is a key to unlock the full potential of any board." —**Marc Bitzer, Chairman and CEO of Whirlpool Corporation, Board Member BMW Group**

"Building effective teams is never easy, and certainly not at the top where egos loom large, pressure is intense, and time scarce. Based on his in-depth knowledge of the theory and practice of leadership, Thomas Sieber gives chairs, CEOs, and directors the tools to overcome these challenges—in the boardroom and beyond."—**Iris Bohnet, Albert Pratt Professor of Business and Government, Harvard Kennedy School, Author of *What Works***

"The journey to become a board member teaches us a set of abilities and attitudes that are not necessarily adequate to act as a value-creating board member. Thomas Sieber's book 'Navigating the Human Side of Boardroom Interactions: Improving Relationships at the Top' brings research, conceptual frameworks, and, more importantly, lots of practical ideas and suggestions to grow as a board member and generate an excellent (authentic and open) group dynamics in the boardroom."—**Claudia Elisa, Chairwoman at Roldão Atacadista and Grupo Cassol and Board member at IBGC (Brazilian Institute of Corporate Governance), Tupy SA and Even SA**

"This book is meticulously researched and informed by many years of real-life experience at a major Swiss company. It provides invaluable insight and practical guidance on the management of board relationships."—**Robert Hingley, Chairman of The Law Debenture Corporation plc and Chairman of Euroclear UK and International Limited**

"What most struck me reading Thomas Sieber's book was his rare ability to blend the academic theory of leadership with real-life experience of senior management in the corporate world. His impressive credentials result in guidance that is both soundly reasoned and easily translated to everyday management situations. His argument is clear—if we could just learn to stop leaving our humanity at the door of the boardroom and take simple steps to be honest and authentic, we could unlock a staggering amount of latent potential. His practical suggestions feel achievable, being deeply rooted in understanding how things work today at the top."—**Jennifer Hogan, Coach, Founder, Sakura Consulting & Development LLC**

"The interaction of board members with the executive team takes, all too often, the form of a Greek chorus. Too much groupthink—and a lack of courage in asking tough questions—contributes to poor board performance. To better understand the psychological dynamics at work—to make boards better functioning entities—board members, aspiring board members, and managers are advised to read Thomas Sieber's book 'Navigating the Human Side of Boardroom Interactions: Improving Relationships at the Top." It will greatly increase their effectiveness.'—**Manfred F. R. Kets De Vries, Distinguished Clinical Professor of Leadership Development and Organizational Change, INSEAD, Fontainebleau & Singapore**

"Thomas Sieber's book 'Navigating the Human Side of Boardroom Interactions' offers a thrilling fine-grained analysis of boardroom dynamics and valuable new insights into the business world that only the fewest know. Still, when it comes to breaking the silence in teams, the recommendations introduced are highly relevant to all of us."—**Markus Schoebel, Industrial Organizational Psychologist, Senior Lecturer at University Basel**

"A much-needed book. The real job of a Chair and the board members is far from clear. Our history and our egos stand in our way to opening up and

improving our interactions at the top. Thomas Sieber's book is an amazing guide, full of real-life knowledge, bold in its fresh and candid look, and easy to read on top of that. Do yourself and your board a favor and READ THIS BOOK!"—**Ricardo Senerman, Chairman Sencorp**

"Reading this remarkable book with its stimulating, immensely thoughtful observations on the human side of boardroom interactions, I felt that this handily compact treasury should not be buried in the briefcases of board members only. Its findings offer a clear-eyed view of the impact of human feelings and reactions on the success of any professional undertaking. For me, the book is a must read for all young professionals—all my adult kids will get it as a present."—**Juergen Sieger, former partner of Freshfields and Cleary Gottlieb Steen & Hamilton and former multiple Chairman and board member (i.a. 1. FC Köln)**

"The tone of the top of a company is key. The effectiveness of its message and subsequent results strongly depend on the competency of its leader(s) to be willing to listen, ask, learn and adapt to change. This book combines refreshing and valuable insights from the author as a board insider and leaders around the globe."—**Marguerite Soeteman Reijnen, Chairwoman of the Executive Board at Aon Holdings**

"How we manage our professional relationships at the top, particularly with members of public boards, is critical for good corporate governance. Learning to talk openly about our challenges and developing practical solutions to overcome obstacles is an area of great potential. Thomas combines his experience as a former executive and executive coach with insights from leaders around the world, culminating in a book that will undoubtedly help leaders better manage themselves and their relationships."—**Chris Wei, Former Executive Chairman, Asia & Global Chairman, Digital, Aviva**

"Thomas has very successfully bundled his extensive real-life and 'close combat' knowhow on a key topic that has, so far, not had the attention it truly deserves: dynamics in boards. I have thoroughly enjoyed reading the book, full of to-the-point examples and practical tips. I have learned a lot from Thomas ... once again. Thank you, Thomas."—**Gert De Winter, Group CEO Baloise Holding**

"This book perfectly highlights how to develop a trusted relationship between the board of directors and the executive board. Such a foundation is needed to reap the benefit of different opinions—both internal and external— to make informed decisions on a company's future strategy. Following the profound and easily accessible guidance of Thomas's book about 'the human side of boardroom interaction,' boards and executive management find resilient ways to successfully address content issues—in a less restrictive and controlled manner—with openness and trust, which I firmly believe will maximize longterm value for the organization and the shareholders who appointed them."—**Pia Tischhauser, Senior Partner and Managing Director, Member of the Group Executive Committee, Boston Consulting Group**

Description

The interactions between Chairs, board members, CEOs, and top management are crucial to a company's success. Understanding the *human dimension* is essential in forming productive one-to-one relationships, relationships within and between teams. We (consciously or unconsciously) assume that avoiding the muddy territory of dealing with personal issues is appropriate. The personalities at the top, their prior success, and their surroundings are for once not a door opener to actively pursuing and working on their professional relationships.

The author explores what those board members need *to form a team* —as unique as their setup may be. Being caught between two strong forces—the Chair and the executive board—makes it difficult for board members to navigate the complex web of boardroom relations. It is widely accepted that forming a high-functioning team takes time, attention, and effort—a given for management teams but not yet the reality for board teams.

The *Chair's role* in forming a board team and developing a robust relationship with the CEO is crucial. The position of the Chair comes with considerable power, which sometimes has to be used. However, Chairs should have a "coaching" attitude: their main job is to make the CEO successful.

The author looks at *all the interactions at the top*. Based on around 60 interviews worldwide and extensive personal experience, he provides "do's" and "don't" to support board members and managers in reflecting on how best to interact.

Keywords

board interactions; the role of the Chair; Chair/CEO relationship; board dynamics; board reviews; board evaluation; team conflicts; high-performing teams; joint board reflection; building trust; forming a team; leadership; psychological safety; vulnerability; speaking up; taking risks; board of directors; executive board; board culture; managing board relations; board coaching; board independence; board engagement

Contents

List of Figures and Tables

Preface

We build too many walls and not enough bridges.

—Isaac Newton

Leadership is not a person or position. It's a complex moral relationship between people based on trust, obligation, commitment, emotion and a shared vision of a good.

—Joanne Ciulla

In a business environment that is more disruptive than ever, the board's role is not just to avoid scandals and comply with regulations: it is to shape strategy for the company, and support and challenge the management. As a result, boards will increasingly have more intense interactions with the executive board.

If boards want to head consciously into this more *active role*, they will have to invest more time in their performance and functioning as a team and in how they interact with the CEO and management.

As successful people in a part-time role, board members usually want to get along. So they may shy away from critical issues; we all want to protect ourselves and our relationships. We take a lot for granted, and a lot is assumed. The consequence is that we are not playing to win; rather, we are playing not to lose.

A more active board will lead to more debates and conflicts, putting greater focus on how we manage *the complex relational web at the top of companies*. The better we know and like ourselves and the less self-absorbed we are, the better we can deal with others. Neuroscience shows that if we feel insecure and anxious, our brain narrows our perception to deal predominantly in self-defense mode, limiting our awareness—not a promising area for board members, or senior management.

To work at our best, we need trusted relationships; to gain trust, we need time together and to share ourselves (vulnerability); to take inter-personal risks (psychological safety), we need to feel safe, and we need to know that speaking up and asking questions is a desired behavior (explicit encouragement). On this basis, we will be able to talk about and feel more at ease with our roles and develop resilient relationships. Instead of wasting resources on self-protection, we can listen attentively, ask good questions, build on each other's contributions, and have the courage to challenge others.

If, additionally, we honestly reflect upon our behavior, we will learn and improve individually, and as a team. Such an environment is no guarantee for success, but it will undoubtedly increase the chances.

The book will help you to better understand what a board team needs and how we can improve relationships at the top. I am convinced that we all have boundless untapped potential—if we are courageous enough to lower our shields and be more human.

I offer many insights for anyone who interacts with boards, but mainly for Chairs, board members, CEOs, and top management. The book is based on my own experiences—mainly as an executive board member, a Chair, a member of different boards, and secretary of the board of directors; a combination of around 60 interviews with Chairs, ordinary board members, and CEOs; my INSEAD thesis about "Improving Board Dynamics and Open Dialogue: How Speaking Up Could Transform Corporate Boards"; and an extensive literature review.

I was prepared to write this book at the Harvard Business School, where I had been admitted as a research fellow with Professor Amy Edmondson as my academic sponsor. The COVID-19 pandemic changed my plans, and I wrote the book at home in Switzerland. Our new "Zoom" culture made it easier to arrange interviews worldwide and recognize that, without minimizing cultural and legal differences, we all are foremost human beings with a need for appreciation, belonging, and inclusion. The body of thought of this book can be applied *cum grano salis* for boards anywhere. Suppose we had the willingness to learn to manage ourselves and our interactions with others. We would get to know ourselves and others better and improve our relationships at the top, benefiting ourselves, our businesses, and our broader environment. The potential is there; we just have to grasp it.

Acknowledgments

The book is about the human side of interactions between board members and management. As secretary of a board of directors early on in my career, I was involved in board matters; probably, in contrast to my educational background as a lawyer, the less formal and less visible issues attracted me the most. Over time and with more experience in different roles and functions with boards, the more potential I saw in improving the interactions within a board and between the board and the management. That laid out the soil for this book.

The seeds for its content were provided by interviews with Chairs and CEOs of 60 different companies around the world. The female share was almost one-third. I express my gratitude to those senior executives who opened up and shared personal insights—in many cases to a stranger they had never talked to before. While COVID-19 prevented me from spending a much-anticipated fellowship year at Harvard with my family, it also made those Zoom calls more natural. During a period when one could not travel nor easily meet friends, I was somewhat connected to the world by conducting interviews with executives in Australia, Austria, Brazil, Canada, Chile, China, Croatia, Denmark, France, Germany, India, Italy, Japan, Kenya, Netherlands, New Zealand, Philippines, Russia, Spain, Singapore, South Africa, South Korea, Switzerland, Turkey, the United Kingdom, and the United States. I express my gratitude to all those who helped me to get interested Chairs and CEOs to interview, mainly Pia Tischhauser and my friends from wave25.com.

Interestingly, only a few board members declined a request for an interview demonstrating a willingness or maybe even a need for reflection time about those more personal questions.

In the writing and review process, I got valuable feedback from Darko Cesar, Ellen Salwen, Gert de Winter, Jürgen Sieger, Markus Schöbel, Mila de Bie, Ramona Dobler, Reto Diezi, Robert Hingley, and Wendy Giardina.

The person who is most closely connected to the book is a new friend I never met physically. Jen Hogan—an ex-manager and now a successful business coach—and I were in the same peer group for our virtual coaching education. She appointed herself to be the chairwoman of my publishing project—a title she fully deserves. She edited, shortened, rewrote—she simply made my book better and was even there when I had to vent and showed then all her coaching strength.

Shelagh Aitken edited the book at a later stage in an efficient, and sensitive manner which calmed my nerves not to lose control over the content.

The team at Business Expert Press with Scott Isenberg, Charlene Kronstedt and Ed Stone as well as the Exeter team supported and helped me throughout the publishing journey.

Finally, my wife Ruth and our two almost adult children, Olivia and Gian, deserve acknowledgment for their never-ending support; it started by letting me have the nicest office to work in at home; they worked on charts and graphs where my main quality was to tell how it could be improved and provided emotional and technical support when the computer was not smart enough to figure out what I wanted it to do. The content of the book—managing relations—offered food for many dinner conversations.

Introduction

The well-run group is not a battlefield of egos.

—Lao Tzu

You don't develop courage by being happy in your relationships every day. You develop it by surviving difficult times and challenging adversity.

—Epicurus

He/his refers to the Chair, while *she/her* refers to the CEO. I have chosen this convention because the CEO is the most important position within a company. The Chair is the head of the board of directors, while the CEO is the head of the executive board.

BM: Stands for board member's quote from my interviews: I don't distinguish between Chairs, board members, or CEOs. If I believe the specifics are relevant, then I point it out.

Relationships Are Hard Work. According to Stephen Covey (1989/2020), "many of the problems in organizations stem from *relationship difficulties* at the very top." This is consistent with my own experience as a board and executive board member. In researching this book, I conducted 60 interviews with Chairs, board members, and CEOs around the globe. Overall, they painted a picture of thoughtful, reflective personalities, somewhat reluctant to use their insights and reflections to work on their professional relationships.

Why? Because the business world, especially at the top, is not (yet) an environment where it comes naturally to work on those relationships, on interpersonal issues; it simply seems too personal.

BM: Showing vulnerability sounds like an oasis of well-being, which I do not consider necessary.

Several Chairs stated that "walking the talk" is more important than "the talk."

> BM: *The daily evidence demonstrates the trust that you act and behave as you claim to do and not by talking about it.*

Fewer Assumptions, More Questions? While I couldn't agree more that "walking the talk" is fundamental and "paper is patient," the crucial relationship between Chair and CEO often does not work as it should. I argue that the business world, especially at the highest levels, would be a different place and deliver better results, by assuming less, asking more (personal) questions, and sharing (ourselves) honestly.

> BM: *I just assumed something, and then I found out much later that the CEO was heavily disappointed.*

Even when we reflect and doubt our assumptions, we seldom address personal issues: it feels uncomfortable. Shying away from potential conflict is easier in the short term but generally stores up a future problem. The uneasy feeling festers, setting the ground for growing irritation, like a weed that is not pulled out early and chokes the plants around it.

In the interviews, I often was confronted with statements from Chairs like:

> BM: *I am a reflective, responsible, and considerate person; that's how I act toward the CEO; I hope she appreciates that and acts accordingly. Sometimes, it works; if it doesn't work, then the CEO needs to go.*

This drastic, fatalistic attitude is in sharp contrast to how financial or strategic questions are handled: these topics, being more factual and less emotional, tend to be handled more thoroughly and objectively. What potential for our company and personal growth is being sacrificed when we only superficially touch the human side of our interactions?

A Successful Chair–CEO Relationship Depends on Qualities in Short Supply at the Top. We know that "walking the talk" is fundamental to build trust. Still, we should be willing to display self-disclosure (Kets de Vries 2011), show vulnerability (Brown 2018) to talk about our needs, and ask about the need of others (Stanier 2016). Such an attitude needs courage, self-esteem, reflection, and a deep-rooted interest in human beings. It also requires readiness to give up control during a conversation and willingness to take risks, not just play it safe.

Giving up control and showing vulnerability seems especially hard for Chairs and CEOs. Typically, a proven track record is necessary to be elected to such powerful positions; there are often "alpha animals" in those roles. It can be argued that if you have reached the top, there should be less need to impress and pretend; however, we are all human, and our search for affirmation does not decrease because we have received it in the past. Once at the top, you are often surrounded by people who tell you what they think you want to hear, muffling true sentiment. This does not increase either your self-awareness or your awareness of others' needs. In this situation, neither the outer environment, including media coverage, capital market pressure, challenging market environment, nor the inner personal environment supports the blossoming of the Chair and CEO's crucial relationship.

The higher you climb the professional ladder, the more experience you have, the more you are confident in your wisdom, and the more you take for granted. You are less inclined to behaviors that foster awareness and growth, challenge certain assumptions, listen, understand a different perspective, and even learn. We become used to having all the answers. It is especially expected that we have the answers as we progress to the top. Argyris (1991), in his article "Teaching Smart People How to Learn," stated that past success does not increase your readiness to learn.

Keltner (2016) used the term "power paradox" to describe how leaders gain influence through empathy and similar practices but lose those skills as they gain power.

It is not surprising that many interviewees were cautious about entering the personal field of working on meaningful relationships. Questioned about what hinders them from acting differently, a typical answer was:

BM: People usually have more trouble setting boundaries if they're getting too friendly.

BM: I'm playing to my instinct. While I have no problem setting boundaries, it is not easy to let people in. I just did something in our interview which was in line with my natural inclination and rationalized it.

The Need for Objectivity and Distance Can Be a Smokescreen. There are sound reasons for some degree of distance between the Chair and the CEO. Suppose the Chair and CEO were to get too close: all the issues could be agreed upon in advance of the board meeting, so there would be no serious challenge or debate between the two. The checks and balances that are fundamental to the objective and independent role of the board would be endangered. Board members would quickly feel excluded, not to mention afraid that the Chair and the CEO had not found the appropriate distance.

Those fears can be a reasonable barrier to relationship building; however, they are often just a pretext. Finding a balance between opening up and conserving appropriate boundaries can be challenging. The default mechanism at the top leans clearly toward boundaries: peers readily reciprocally confirm why we should stick to that attitude.

What Exactly Is the Role of the Board of Directors? The Chair–CEO relationship is the most prominent, but the same is true for any other (business) relationship. Almost no relationship is one-to-one, and certainly not in the business world. At the top of the company, we have relationships within a team, and between members of different teams, and we have to balance the needs of all. The Chair, for example, has to manage his relationship with the CEO, the executive board team, and with his team—*the board of directors.*

Boards have a problematic starting point. In most cases, boards have little true room to maneuver; they are confronted with high and sometimes conflicting expectations. Investors expect an above-average return; the public and the media expect a sustainable, successful business model, good corporate citizenship, no mistakes, and, in particular, greedy managers tamed. Public opinion and employees tend to overestimate the board's influence, as a mysterious and unknown body, called the "black box" in the literature.

The reality is that board members are caught between two forces: the Chair and the executive board. The latter has to run the company and benefits from having a straightforward task. A strong Chair is crucial for a company, not just in the formal definition of the role but also in his personality and history.

The question then emerges: What tasks are left for the board? What can a board member contribute?

BM: I am a proud board member and proud to belong to this group. Please believe me if I tell you that everyone, especially those with operational experience, asks themselves critically in such a body: What is our contribution? The added value in management is much higher than on the board. You have undoubtedly heard the saying of Hermann Josef Abs, Head of Deutsche Bank, in the 1950s and 1960s. "What is the difference between a doghouse and a board of directors? The doghouse is for the dog; the board of directors is for the cat." I have never seen the board come up with an ingenious idea: develop the idea of taking the company a quantum leap forward. And that's what I ask myself: How can I, and how can we as a board team, add value to the company?

What role is the Chair willing to give to his board?

BM: I sense that the Chair prefers not to have too many debates, and I act accordingly.

And what is the board members' perception of the Chair?

BM: It does not feel right if I speak up against the Chair; it feels disloyal, and I don't want to risk my relationship with the Chair.

How open is the executive board to include the board of directors in shaping the company's future, not just in nodding agenda points?

BM: I often observed a kind of cynicism in the management. Oh, those board members don't understand the business and want to know things that are irrelevant and cause us more work that isn't adding any value.

Maybe the Chair wants to have an active board but has doubts about how to contribute.

BM: I would like to make a difference and have an impact, but I am not sure how I can add value; so, I chose to be silent.

As a former CEO, you are used to telling others how things should be done and carry on with that behavior as a board member.

BM: I know the business, I want to have an impact, and I will make a difference here.

This small selection of statements is just a few examples of board members' thinking. All the behaviors have a reason but also potential dysfunctional effects.

What exacerbates the situation is that we are often unaware of our actions or inactions. They are below conscious awareness, especially if we have not reflected on our roles or discussed the anxieties that can come with a board position.

Being a board member appears to be an excellent position with obvious benefits (prestige, salary, belonging), but board members still have needs, concerns, and fears. If those needs are not met, or concerns and fears are not addressed, they may lead to dysfunctional behaviors.

Part I of this book covers the board's position, team members' needs, and the *Chair's role*. While the CEO's role is challenging, especially in an increasingly dynamic and complex environment, her responsibility is clear-cut. What a Chair should do (or not do), however, is less obvious and visible. While the main objective is clearly to make the company, the CEO, and her team successful, the Chair's role is less clear-cut.

The Chair plays the central role in the team-building process of the board. It starts with the crucial question:

What Does the Chair Want From His Team? In theory, the Chair intends to have a strong team, fighting for the best outcome, where anybody can speak openly and make an impact. Such a board sounds excellent on paper, but in reality, as a Chair, managing it could be a daunting task: strong teams inevitably lead to tensions and conflicts. While this would be in the company's interests, as multiple opinions contribute to the best thinking overall, it would be unsurprising for a Chair to (sub) consciously seek an easier life. So, as a Chair, you may see the rationale for conflicts and debates, but default to a tamer, more relaxed board.

Chair positions are filled by *alpha animals*, individuals with successful track records, strong presence, and opinions. One of my questions for you is: Does the Chair, or do other board members, genuinely have an appetite to have a board where intense debates can occur? If so, what can they do to create that culture? What can they do to foster a constructive challenge and growth atmosphere so that the executive board looks forward to the next board meeting instead of seeing it as a hurdle?

> *BM: My vision is that the executive board is looking forward to the next board meeting because they feel appreciated, supported, and challenged simultaneously. We all learn together for the benefit of the company. If this happens, I have won as a Chair.*

The Multidimensional Role of the Chair. The *Chair's role* is crucial in developing such a culture and delivering that vision. The Chair manages a web of relational issues; he leads the board; interacts with senior management, in particular the CEO; and talks to regulators, investors, and the media.

The role of the Chair calls for self-restraint. He can potentially strengthen his reputation, self-esteem, and appreciation from the board, maybe even from the public, should he choose to intervene vis-à-vis management. However, such a decision would almost inevitably be at a cost to the company and its management team. The Chair has to think carefully before overruling the CEO: what looks strong and decisive for him personally can easily damage the company's well-being. The judgment to make the call in the ultimate best interest asks much from the Chair, calling for a reflective personality.

The way Chairs are selected aggravates the challenge. A former, experienced Chair said:

> *BM: Let's call a spade a spade. Chairpersons are often chosen for celebrity and relationship reasons. The insight that the central task of the*

Chair demands qualities in respect to the group dynamic and the group psychological leadership issues of the board and the interaction with the management is not part of the mainstream knowledge or consciousness of the people who propose the Chairs.

In *Part I*, I suggest an ideal Chair profile before I take a closer look in *Part II* at the *interactions at the top*. Based on my interviews, literature, and my own experience, reporting for many years to Chairs and CEOs, I have developed recommendations on improving our working relationships at the top while simultaneously building effective teams. In each of those chapters, I include examples from my interviews and personal experiences. I provide "do's" and "don'ts" to help Chairs, board members, and management reflect on how to interact.

The book ends with *Part III* about *reflections for the boardroom*. I distinguish between self-reflection, reflection-in-action, and joint-reflection after the action, as well as reflection workshops for board reviews, including behavioral traps to avoid and tips for conducting each session.

Board members are in a unique position to provide feedback and reflect together. In the quantitative part of my INSEAD study (Sieber 2019), I found that the board of directors' joint reflections were the most significant drivers for the boardroom's psychological safety and voice behavior.

PART I

The Board of Directors

CHAPTER 1

The Picture From the Past

The best time to plant a tree is twenty years ago. The second-best time is today.

—Chinese Proverb

Grant me the serenity to accept the things I cannot change, the courage to change things I can, and the wisdom to know the difference.

—Reinhold Niebuhr

Boards Were Passive and Formal Institutions

Boards were traditionally considered to be formal and passive institutions (Mace 1971). The prevailing wisdom was to get along and not expose yourself (Sonnenfeld, Kusin, and Walton 2013). As one CEO describes the phenomenon: "In the boardroom, the thinking is: 'You have to be equal. Don't be overwhelming or dominant, don't hurt feelings, and don't take someone's chair'" (Sonnenfeld et al. 2013). So, rather than playing to win, you play to avoid losing:

BM: I am in—I want to get along. No reason to expose myself.

As a traditional board member, you may be delighted to belong to a prestigious circle providing external admiration and decent financial benefit, especially considering the time spent on the board's mandate.

You were likely chosen to join the board by a Chair who knows you well. You could therefore feel stronger loyalty to the Chair than to the company. In the event of doubts about raising your voice on a critical issue, this could make you more likely to choose to be silent.

Indeed, my quantitative research (Sieber 2019a) confirmed that. The relational silence motive—not to speak up because you want to protect a relationship—is a strong motivator to remain silent. On this basis, boards who wish to debate should restrain themselves from recruiting from the "old boys" network.

> *BM: Sometimes board members are too good buddies of the Chair and therefore they are not ready to "rain on his parade."*

From an insider perspective and past experiences, it's unsurprising that a strong Chair and management prefer a restrained board, where board members have prestige without putting in too much effort. Obligations outside of board member roles more central to their careers are another reason not to engage at full throttle. A likely outcome, then, is a somewhat passive board. Describing such a picture is a gross generalization. Still, I would be surprised if many board members disagreed with my overall painting of the reality of board members from the past.

The Wrong Focus on Formal Independence

For a long time, the academic world focused on seemingly quantitative topics like board member demographics and formal independence. A hot topic was the demand to get independent directors on the board. Jensen and Meckling (1976), in their influential agency theory, made the distinction between the "non-independent" (*insider*) director and the "independent" (*outsider*) director on boards. The general assumption was that independent directors lead to better board performance; "independence" meant being an outside director with a tenure of less than a specified number of years.

Corporate Governance Guidelines of proxy advisors like ISS or Glass Lewis stress formal independence. As an example, Ethos (2018), a Swiss advisor, had written—promisingly—in its proxy voting guidelines that "a person's independence is fundamentally a question of character," only to conclude: "It is thus necessary to evaluate the independence of board members against generally accepted objective criteria," ending in a list of conditions to be fulfilled to qualify as independent. This point neatly shows our propensity to what can be measured, controlled, and even audited. But external parties can hardly address the real issue: *independence in mind,* to which I will return in Chapter 5.

Around the turn of the millennium, major crises hit the corporate world. A common perception was that those scandals could have been avoided if boards had taken their responsibilities more seriously. Lawmakers and regulators reacted: corporate governance was the salvation. I was general counsel and secretary of a board of a publicly listed company at that time, so to a certain extent formed its corporate governance structure. Corporate governance regulation and, quite often, "soft" law brought many good initiatives that it is hard to imagine today's business world without. However, the new rules and regulations also led to a checkbox mentality, focusing on legal and structural issues since the lawmakers had no other access to board rooms.

Unfortunately, new scandals were still hitting the corporate world. Companies like Enron who had a stellar reputation and shining corporate governance—at least on paper—went bankrupt. What went wrong?

As it transpires, complying with governance requirements advocated by governing bodies, proxy advisors, and shareholder groups was insufficient (Griffin, Larcker, Miles, and Tayan 2017). Finkelstein and Mooney (2003) conclude that "academics, consultants, and reformers pursue the holy grail of independence" without success because they tend to look at the "usual suspects," such as formal independence, which ultimately seem to be irrelevant.

Research has found no systematic relationship between either the board's independence based on formal criteria (Dalton, Daily, Ellstrand, and Johnson 1998) or tenure (for an overview of research, Johnson, Schnatterly, and Hill 2013) and company performance. Stevenson and Radin (2015) concluded that formal "independence does not necessarily translate into the ability to influence others or result in the independence of decision making."

While the law encounters significant hurdles in accessing inner dynamics and the often-hidden and unconscious sides of the decision-making process, the following quote from the Swiss Supreme Court (BGE 4a 129/2013 E 4.3) is remarkable: "It cannot be excluded that the wish of the Chair influenced the decision of the board to grant the loan and that the board members felt obliged or maybe did not want to risk their board seat." The quote raises specifically the question of whether a board member is unwilling to risk his or her seat and, therefore, does not act as a genuinely independent director.

A Board Is a Group of Human Beings
With a Social Contract

Researchers (Pettigrew 1992 or Finkelstein and Hambrick 1996) demanded that future research pay attention to the board's behavior and decision-making process long ago instead of a demography–outcome approach. Lawrence (1997) pointedly states: "Traditional demographic indicators leave us at a loss as to the real psychological and social processes that are driving executive behavior." The output of boards is mainly cognitive. Therefore, Forbes and Milliken (1999, p. 492) suggest "that the effectiveness of boards is likely to depend heavily on social-psychological processes, particularly those pertaining to group participation and interaction, the exchange of information and critical discussion."

Roberts, McNulty, and Stiles (2005) argue that actual board effectiveness "depends upon the behavioral dynamics of a board, and how the web of interpersonal and group relationships" functions. Depending on board composition, behavior can trigger very different reactions, making it hard to draw the line between good and bad for the board. Looking at those intragroup dynamics—often referred to as "soft" issues—is less accessible and controllable but provides "the most significant learning opportunity for boards" (Griffin et al. 2017).

Frustrated with the superficial thinking of the industry around governance, William Donaldson says: "The most important part is the least examined: the board is a social entity. And the human beings on it—they act like human beings do in groups." Donaldson is surprised that more work has not been done to illuminate "the social contract within a board" (Donaldson; cited in Sonnenfeld et al. 2013).

The public and the media have zero, and lawmakers and regulators have minimal access to boards' inner dynamics. But with pressure to tame boards and managers, we should not be surprised that lawmakers were focused on formal issues which can be controlled and audited.

What about the investors? More prominent investors can gain access to board members, and the topic of corporate culture has finally got the investor's attention. Culture is critical to a company's long-term success, and boards must play their role in defining and shaping it (State Street

2019; BlackRock 2019). The Prudential Regulation Authority of the Bank of England (2018) also stresses the Chair and the CEO's leading roles in shaping the right culture. We cannot talk about corporate culture without looking closely at the culture and interaction both within the board of directors and with the executive board. As a famous proverb states, "The fish begins to stink at the head."

But what about the board members themselves? How keen are Chairs to have real debates in the board room? How ready is management to have a board team that asks questions? As I have already stressed, human beings, and board members, in particular, tend to shy away from personal issues or conflicts. Still, boards should tackle their responsibility to address the crucial problems that cannot be easily regulated.

The Challenge of Change in the Boardroom

Discussion of behavioral issues in business is becoming more common, even on boards. Many interviewees were open to discussing those issues, but the current board reality still lags behind, and western culture does little to support openness.

As Schein and Schein (2021, p. 68) put it:

> We see U.S. culture reinforcing tacit assumptions of pragmatism, individualism, competition, and status through achievement. These assumptions introduce a strong bias for getting the job done, which, combined with individualism, leads to a relative devaluing of relationship building, teamwork, and collaboration, except as means to the end of task accomplishment. Given those cultural biases, doing and telling are all too often valued more than asking, listening and relationship building.

Our "cultural backpack" of how things are done does not support change in the board room. Boards are particularly challenged because they do not operate in a real-time world demanding responsiveness or change, so many things are done "the way they always have been." Organizations, like individuals, are creatures of habit; once a team's rules and behavior patterns have been established, consciously or unconsciously, change is challenging, even if the need for change seems clear, demonstrated in this example paraphrased from Kets de Vries (2011, p. 176):

> Six monkeys were living in a cage; in the middle was a ladder, which led to a bunch of bananas. When the first monkey climbed the ladder and reached the bananas, all other monkeys were sprayed with ice-cold water. This happened whenever a monkey tried to get the bananas. Soon, each monkey who attempted to climb the ladder was stopped by the others. Each new monkey that arrived tried to get to the bananas but was attacked fiercely by the other monkeys. For each new monkey added, a resident monkey was taken out of the cage. It wasn't long before all of the monkeys who had experienced the ice shower were gone. Nevertheless, the norm had been settled, and the monkeys made sure that no new monkey tried to climb the ladder, even if none of the monkeys had ever suffered the icy shower.

New board members will soon learn expected behaviors. Newcomers are usually indoctrinated by existing members, perpetuating the status quo. Knowing that change does not come easily, especially if the topics are under the surface and more psychodynamic, boards have to make the conscious choice to address how they work together and interact with management. The example of the monkeys is pretty similar to the board room reality. Newcomers enter—the cage of the board room—and are educated about how to behave.

The executive board deals with most of the outer environment's challenges and drives overall change in the company. The boards of directors have to reflect upon where change is needed at the board level and how interaction with management occurs. Talking about such changes is not easy and can feel uncomfortable. Without robust relationships between board members, it is a conversation that can only be held at a superficial level, if at all.

I am not a change enthusiast per se, but I believe that the board of directors can make a difference if they are willing to work *as a team*, creating an effective team culture where *independence of mind* can be nurtured.

Boards have to realize that to accomplish more challenging tasks, they have to invest in their relationships; they have to take the time to *form a team*: to talk about their roles, expectations, fears, and concerns. I will look at the board of directors as a team in the next chapter before I look in Chapter 3 at the role of the Chair, who is crucial in developing board culture.

CHAPTER 2

A Team With Needs

Teamwork is the ability to work together toward a common vision. The ability to direct individual accomplishments toward organizational objectives. It is the fuel that allows common people to attain uncommon results.

—Andrew Carnegie

He who mistrusts most, should be trusted least.

—Theognis of Megara

The Board of Directors as a Special Team

Western culture predominantly focuses on the individual; just look at most corporate reward systems. While you get better financial remuneration if the company's results are better, you rarely have specific goals regarding team behavior. Indeed, research on board governance and board behavior focuses almost exclusively on the individual, not the board as a team (Charas 2015). Still, it is *teams* that are the foundation of society and community (Schein, in the foreword to Edmondson 2012) or with Kets de Vries (2011): "The 21st century will be the age of teams."

Edmondson (2012), in her book about "teaming," provides a broader context. Industrialization replaced the structure of self-reliance with small, repetitive steps, making mass production possible and leading to a top-down, command-and-control management style. But today's knowledge-based industry demands more *collaboration, innovation, and organizational learning* (Edmondson 2012). This calls for more interaction between the individual by speaking up, asking questions, and sharing ideas.

Kets de Vries (2011, p. 6) defines teams as

"specific groups of people with (it is hoped) complementary skills and abilities who join together to cooperate. People in a team possess a high degree of interdependence geared toward the achievement of a common goal or completion of a task for which we hold one another mutually accountable."

In my interviews, there was no dispute about the board being a team:

*BM: The whole point of a board is that you bring different perspectives and different views together, and you're able to debate that in a **team**. I recognize and respect what it is that you bring, which is different from what I bring.*

*BM: In a healthy board environment, board members are encouraged and free to express their views, and nobody is going to think that is stupid, and nobody is going to belittle them. You can only do that if your **board is a team**.*

*BM: If you are not willing to have diversity around the table combined with the confidence to express your opinion, you are not **a team in reality**, and then you just have a board because it is a legal requirement.*

*BM: It is essential not only to have the expertise but also to have people who can work together and **play as a team**: for example, in a soccer team, you cannot have 11 stars. We're taking our time to understand if we have a good balance among all members, so that we can get along well and challenge each other where needed.*

For a long time, board research has ignored the team perspective (Vandewaerde, Voordeckers, Lambrechts, and Bammens 2011). But considering the board of directors as a team is not controversial, provided we remember that there are fundamental differences between a board and a top management team.

A board team is an outlier in the business world.

- Boards control management and monitor and influence strategy but do not generally implement decisions (Fama and Jensen 1983). If you are not entirely happy with a decision as a board member, it is easier to live with because it does not affect your daily life.
- Since it is only a part-time job, board members may be emotionally less engaged (Forbes and Milliken 1999), seeking less exposure and accepting decisions without challenging them.
- Board meetings are formal and take place with many participants. Members spend little time together.
- By taking risks and speaking up, an employee can either lose or win respect and attention from his superiors (Burris 2012). However, a board member has less to gain, at least in the short term, except strengthening his/her self-esteem.
- If a board's selection process still involves "handpicking" driven by the Chair, board members are likely reluctant to speak up.
- You may just be happy to be in a prestigious position. The status of the organization and its impact on your reputation may be satisfaction enough, so there is no need to take risks (Lencioni 2002).

As described in the introduction, boards are awkwardly placed between the Chair and the executive management. It may not be apparent how they can add value and what is expected of them can be opaque; in a part-time job, the readiness to discuss roles and expectations may be further limited (see the recommendations in Chapter 5).

The aforementioned points could explain why board members, who often have had a successful career and enough self-confidence to act courageously, counterintuitively choose not to take risks and remain silent.

Being aware that board teams are different from management teams, they nevertheless should be *considered as teams* and their members should be treated as human beings within a team; but whether they *perform* as a team is a different story. In research conducted by Finkelstein and Mooney (2003), 84 percent of the interviewed board members stated that working together as a team is crucial for its success. However, a study by Heidrick and Struggles (2010) revealed an intriguing picture: while 90 percent of the board members considered themselves to be very effective as individuals, only 30 percent rated the overall board's performance as very effective.

I agree with Hambrick (2007, p. 341):

> Boards are teams—even if they are special in many circumstances—formed by human beings with all our strengths and weaknesses—susceptible to fatigue, boredom, jealousy, cognitive biases, social preening, and selfishness.

In the following two sections, I will look first at what great teams do and then at what teams need to act as great team.

What Do Great Teams Do?

In this section, I will use a chart (Figure 2.1) to assemble step by step what great teams do. Step 1 shows two major topics, "trust and conflict" and how they are linked to each other.

Figure 2.1 Trust and conflict

Step 1/6: Nurture Trust and Acknowledge Conflicts

Let's start with trust. Everybody seems to agree that *trust* is the essential ingredient for a relationship that functions well. My interviewees concurred:

BM: Once you have established trust, you can have an open debate.

When we talk about trust, we usually think in relation to somebody else. This is in line with the overall understanding of trust as an interpersonal concept. A widely accepted definition of trust is provided by Rousseau, Sitkin, Burt, and Camerer (1998): "Trust is a psychological state comprising the intention to accept vulnerability based upon positive expectations of the intentions or behaviours of another."

Besides this relational component, trust has another dimension as well. If we are to trust others, we need to *trust ourselves*. In his book about the speed of trust (2006), Stephen M.R. Covey starts with the question, "Do I trust myself and am I someone others can trust?" These two questions boil down to credibility, which has a character and a competence component. The character part relates to integrity and intent. Integrity consists of congruence, humility, and courage. Intent matters: people often draw conclusions from their inferences, so we have to influence the conclusions of others by being open with our intent. In the business environment, we compete in, we tend to tell and make assumptions rather than being curious and asking (Schein and Schein 2021), which makes disclosing intent crucial. I will come back to those issues when we address the Chair/CEO relationship in Chapter 6. For the moment, it is essential to note that you need to trust yourself to trust others and to inspire people to trust you.

So, how do we build trust?

BM: Trust is demonstrated by the daily evidence you act and behave like you claim to do.

In other words, "walk the talk." If actions do not follow the fine words, it is not "walk the talk." I prefer implicit compliments to explicit ones, which are sometimes formulaic and can make me suspicious.

Trust calls for consistency and integrity. But how long does it take to develop trust? How often do you experience a critical situation where you gain trust because you can observe the desired behavior in the other person? Earning trust through daily evidence, "walk the talk" is great, but what else can we do?

Being curious about your partner's needs is not typical in business circles, even less so sharing your own needs. But how can you trust somebody if they aren't willing to share their concerns and needs? Taking the quote of Theognis of Megara, "he who mistrusts most, should be trusted least," your starting point should be somewhat trustful although not naïve. If you take the proper steps in sharing yourself, hopefully, the other party will follow. Therefore, I invite you to share yourself in doses and observe whether the other side does the same. Trust is mutual. It is built over time with many small steps, but it can be destroyed quickly.

Writing about how to develop trust, Bridges and Bridges (2016) highlight:

- Share yourself honestly—mistrust begins when people are unable to read you.
- Try to extend the trust you place in others a little further than you usually would. Being trusted makes a person more trustworthy, and trustworthy people are more trusting.
- Don't be surprised if your trust-building project is viewed suspiciously. Asking people to let go of their mistrust is like asking them to give up a bit of their self-protection. It does not come easily.

Trust is the grease for all our interactions; a lower level of trust makes our interactions less joyful, authentic, efficient, and more cautious because *we try to avoid conflicts*. Scholars agree that successful teams need to acknowledge that conflict is necessary and productive. Edmondson (2012) points out four behaviors that drive team success: speaking up, collaboration, experimentation, and reflection. I will come back to reflection. The first three behaviors lead to a more active team, triggering more interaction and, consequently, more tensions and conflicts. The fear of conflict is a crucial dysfunction in teams (Lencioni 2002); the best teams need to tackle conflict (Kets de Vries 2011). Or again, from Edmondson (2012): "Leaders who do not grasp the concept that conflict is desirable to teaming, and who do not learn the skills necessary to confront conflict, are destined to fail."

The literature stresses that successful teams need not shy away from conflict, but board teams are especially prone to such an attitude.

According to Edmondson and Smith (2006), we have two options when facing a potentially tricky business discussion. We can either remain silent—often the preferred choice—to preserve our relationships, or we can speak up and risk triggering an emotionally charged debate and our relationships. Board members and managers should not shy away from conflicts. The quiet life has a cost; bad feelings remain latent and omnipresent through nonverbal communication.

In his classic book about the five dysfunctions of a team, Lencioni (2002) mentioned as his most fundamentals points "lack of trust and fear of conflict." The other issues are "lack of commitment," "avoidance of accountability," and "inattention to results." Without trust, you will not engage in passionate and unfiltered debates; a saying goes—*without conflict, no harmony*—because we only seek an artificial harmony by avoiding the necessary conflicts.

The readiness for teams to build trusts and to enter into conflicts appears so prominently in the literature that we should understand some basics about conflicts.

Productive Versus Unproductive Conflict?

Substantial research focuses on the distinction between positive task and negative relational conflict. But how do we recognize if a conflict is a task or a relational conflict? I remember a heated argument from school:

Personal Example

We were arguing about an issue "who had to pay for what" and I had a heated debate with one of my best friends. The teacher interrupted and stated that we were obviously not getting along because of personal issues. The class laughed since his observation was wrong, but he was right to sense something we didn't recognize. Our upbringing had led us to very different views on the same subject. We fought for different values: he for generosity, me for justice. As I had grown up with less money than he did, our fundamental difference in values could be explained easily. But we did not realize it.

This personal example shows what often happens in a business environment: when the debate gets heated, it is labeled as a relational problem in order to put it aside because it feels uncomfortable. Some may resort to rhetoric to cloud issues and disagreements. In my experience, the rhetorically well-equipped are, more often than not, shy about having conflicts.

However, if our values are attacked, even inadvertently, we react strongly (Edmondson 2012) and it may be necessary for somebody to intervene with a good question. It could be that it is not an unproductive relationship conflict that has to be avoided but a value discussion that may be fundamental for the company's future direction. Talking about our own and others' values independently from a heated debate can help a team bond and better manage conflicting views later (see Chapter 3, personality traits of a Chair).

It is certainly helpful for a team to avoid relationship conflicts that negatively affect performance. But if they do, they should be addressed sometime: if relational issues are apparent, they will hinder a team's effectiveness. "Addressed" does not mean that they have to be rolled out in front of the entire board, but they should be dealt with somehow.

A successful team needs to endure tensions and conflicts by "acknowledging emotional reactions openly and exploring what led to them rather than pretending they don't exist" (Edmondson 2012). We learn to suppress feelings rather than act upon them; but by *not* acknowledging our feelings, we may paradoxically act on our feelings when we're least aware of them. As Schein and Schein (2021, p. 101) state: "It is not impulsiveness per se that causes difficulty. It is acting on impulses that are not consciously understood, and hence not evaluated prior to the action, that can get us into trouble."

Fight/Flight or Seeker/Withdrawer

As human beings, we have a natural tendency to respond when challenged with a fight-or-flight response. The better we know ourselves, the easier it is to adjust our default reaction. It also helps to understand the natural tendency of our counterpart, which may be different. Our default response depends heavily on how we were brought up. The overall situation and context also influence how, or at least how strongly, we react. We may show our fight response more strongly at home, whereas we may suppress that inclination with a customer. In any case, it is helpful to recognize via self-observation, feedback, or tests whether you are an avoider or a seeker. While a seeker is eager to engage in disagreements and values directness and honesty, an avoider shies away from disagreement and values harmony. Both are trying to pursue connection: the seeker by attacking, demanding, lecturing, and criticizing (seeking the connection), the avoider by withdrawing, shutting down, and stonewalling (thus preserving the connection). The attacker pushes the withdrawer in a direction that makes the attacker even more upset (for more, see Gershfeld and Sedehi 2021 who describe the cycles in the three basic constellations: attack–withdraw, attack–attack, or withdraw–withdraw, and what we can do to reconnect; also Gallo 2017, with helpful questions to assess yourself). According to Gershfeld and Sedehi (2021), the "withdraw–withdraw cycle" is prevalent in organizations because most managers are averse to conflict.

Cognitive Errors

We have all been in situations where we have decided that our counterpart just does not get it, a view that seems obvious to us. It is good to be aware of two common cognitive errors identified by psychologists: naïve realism and fundamental attribution error (Edmondson 2012).

Naïve realism: People see their views as being more common than they are, which leads us overoptimistically to believe that others share our view; when somebody disagrees, we tend to blame them.

Fundamental attribution error: While we attribute others' shortcomings to their lack of ability or attitude, we do the opposite with our failures and externalize them.

These cognitive errors may explain why we negatively judge others easily and enter into a conflict (fight) or give in without understanding the different perspective (flight).

Knowing that a team needs conflict, that we can get emotional when our values are attacked, and learning about our natural tendency in disputes, and that we are prone to cognitive errors makes it easier to control reactions in a conflict and understand a different perspective, without leaning toward an attitude to avoid any conflicts.

Step 2/6: Feeling Safe and Taking Interpersonal Risks (Psychological Safety)

Edmondson's (1999) line of thinking, closely related to Lencioni's link between trust and conflict, builds on the concept of *psychological safety*, the bridge between trust and conflict, more specifically *between feeling safe and taking interpersonal risks* (Figure 2.2).

Figure 2.2 Psychological safety—feeling safe and taking interpersonal risks

She defined psychological safety—from a team perspective—as "a shared belief held by members of a team that the team is safe for interpersonal risk-taking" (Edmondson 1999). Psychological safety allows individuals to focus on collective goals instead of self-protection (Schein 1993). Edmondson and Lei (2014, p. 31) conclude that "a psychologically safe environment enables divergent thinking, creativity, and risk-taking and motivates engagement in exploratory and exploitative learning, thereby promoting team performance." If this concept were applied to boards as a team, it would provide an ideal description of a functioning board. Since the overwhelming research on psychological safety shows it affects team performance positively and enables organizations to learn (for more, Frazier, Fainshmidt, Klinger, Pezeshkan, and Vracheva 2017; Newman, Donohue and Eva 2017), the challenge must be somewhere else, namely, how to build psychological safety.

Google undertook a project called Aristotle to determine which teams perform best: the results showed that psychological safety was more crucial for a team's performance than anything else (Bergmann and Schaeppi 2016). When team members shared something personal about themselves, they felt more able to speak up on business-related issues (Duhigg 2016). The quantitative part of my INSEAD thesis (Sieber 2019a) confirmed this: sharing private issues increases team members' psychological safety and therefore increases voice behavior.

In a world of constant and ever-increasing change, where network structures are arising, hierarchies are turning flatter, and boundaries are opening up, the ability to adapt and collaborate is becoming more critical. As a result, new boundaries, more psychological than organizational, are needed and perceived individual psychological safety will be an even more critical success factor (Hirschhorn and Gilmore 1992; Krantz 2010).

Step 3/6: Speaking Up

Speaking up is understood as an attitude in which one determines that it is important to address critical issues, even if it brings personal risk (Figure 2.3).

Figure 2.3 Speaking up

However, managers and employees avoid risks and suppress emotions. They put power relations and "peacekeeping ahead of real work," even "suppressing their desire to give constructive criticism"—in short, to speak up (Zaleznik 1997). In an interview about *Why Teams Don't Work*, J. Richard Hackman (2009, p. 105) reflects on the damage incurred by the global financial crisis and invites us to consider the profound impact of failing to speak up:

> One wonders if the crisis in the financial world today would be quite so catastrophic if more people had spoken out in their team meetings about what they knew to be wrongful practices. But again, that brings us back to the hazards of courage. You'd like to think that people who do the courageous right thing and speak out will get their reward on earth as well as in heaven. But you don't always get your reward here on earth.

Many other researchers and professionals have alluded to this same critical issue. In Vuori and Huy's study (2016) on how Nokia lost the smartphone battle, they quote a manager: "I thought that I should point it out, but the thought of challenging made my heart race, and then I just kept quiet." Further evidence is found in Edmondson (2018), where Lutz is quoted as saying that the VW diesel scandal has its root cause in "a culture where performance was driven by fear and intimidation."

This is evidence of the need to speak up in the face of a looming crisis and a tremendous hesitancy—even fear—on the part of those faced with the prospect of verbally challenging the status quo. Fear is an impediment to speaking up, as is obedience to authority figures, learned in our youth and reinforced in most adult institutions (Detert and Trevino 2010 with reference to Milgram 1974). A particular leader's behavior can cause employees to conclude that it is unsafe or futile to speak up (Morrison and Milliken 2000).

Extensive research has been conducted regarding employee silence and voice. Getting employees to voice ideas and thoughts has been recognized as a key driver of high-quality decisions and organizational improvement (e.g., Detert and Edmondson 2011), while silence can lead to failures (e.g., Morrison and Milliken 2000).

When researching "speaking up" in board rooms, one has to look at the extensive research on employee voice and silence (for a broad review, Morrison 2014). Research overwhelmingly indicates that employees choose silence because the likely benefits of speaking up do not outweigh the potential costs (Morrison and Milliken 2000). Silence offers immediate self-protection, while the benefit of voice is uncertain and may occur much later. And the benefit of voice is potentially more for the company or customers than for the individual (Edmondson 2018).

What do we know about the open dialogue—speaking up—in boardrooms? According to a study by Griffin et al. (2017), half of the directors believe that their peers do not express their opinions honestly while management is present; only a quarter believe that board members effectively provide honest and constructive feedback to fellow directors.

A study by Sonnenfeld et al. (2013) revealed that CEOs miss energetic and constructive debates in the boardroom. Knowing that boards are full of powerful, successful, opinionated people, this attitude may be surprising, but learning about the psychology of teams, it is not unexpected (Sonnenfeld et al. 2013).

My INSEAD thesis (Sieber 2019a) focused on whether board members prefer to speak up or remain silent. Can we apply extensive research on employee voice and silence to board members? With a quantitative survey, I tried to see if board members' silence behavior is similar to employees' silence motives. I checked four different silence motives:

- Defensive—fear of negative consequences for oneself
- Diffident—lack of confidence, being shy
- Ineffectual—a taken-for-granted situation, not worth the effort
- Relational—not hurting relationships

Due to the quantitative analysis, I could conclude that those silence motives are also relevant for board members; therefore, the extensive research on employee silence and voice is also applicable to board members.

Speaking up could improve board decisions and prevent liability cases or decisions that hamper the company's reputation, as well as their own.

Speaking up in a boardroom demonstrates that you are willing to take a risk in the form of an intervention, potentially challenging the mainstream, or the perceived general direction, of an issue. It can be also more exploratory, attaching a question mark to a topic. Let's assume the subject of compensation. A proposal for the CEO bonus is on the table. You may have a bad feeling, but everybody else seems to approve the proposal silently. You may ask the question: "Are we doing the right thing here?" Or more: "I have a bad feeling about that package; are we doing the right thing here?"

It is important to note that "speaking up" does not contradict asking or inquiring. Speaking up should not be confused with an attitude of being the knower. It can mean that you are disclosing that you have a gut feeling or that you are asking challenging questions or that you are stating a strong opinion about something.

Boards of directors have to make tough decisions under challenging circumstances. Due to limited time and a relatively large number of participants at meetings, members have to assess whether to make their voices heard or remain silent. The challenge is to find the balance between asking a question, making your point, expressing your views, listening, and functioning as a team of colleagues. Speaking up at the wrong moment can shut down somebody else. So, we should always reflect on whether we should suspend our immediate response to create dialogue. Listening and building on other arguments is a different means of encouragement for somebody else to speak up. As illustrated in Figure 2.4, if we reflect on our behavior (see step 6 in this chapter), speak up, or suspend our thoughts to listen and then build on each other's, we are on an excellent track.

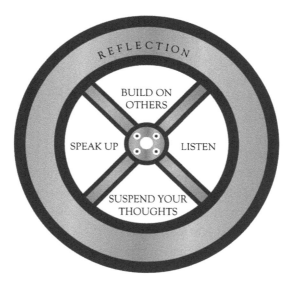

Figure 2.4 Reflection wheel

Step 4/6: Being Encouraged to Speak Up

Readiness to take risks leads to a higher probability of having conflicts. Studies have shown that employees with a greater sense of psychological safety are more willing to express voice (e.g., Detert and Burris 2007; Detert and Trevino 2010). My INSEAD thesis (Sieber 2019a) revealed an exciting result: *psychological safety is necessary but not sufficient for speaking up in board rooms.*

Why would board members feel safe but not speak up? They may not know if speaking up is a desired behavior in the boardroom.

In my quantitative study, only the concept of *dialogue promotion* created the vital link between psychological safety and voice. *Dialogue* promotion and open communication goes back to Bresó, Gracia, Latorre, and Peiró (2008) and describes to what degree open and honest communication occurs within a team and *is promoted*. To put it technically, dialogue promotion acted as a mediator between psychological safety and voice behavior; bluntly, board members may feel safe, but without explicit and repeated encouragement to speak up, they may remain silent. Therefore, the arrow *(being encouraged)* in Figure 2.5 between feeling safe and taking risks is of utmost importance.

Figure 2.5 Being encouraged to speak up

We need to know that asking questions and entering into debates is desired. Without making it explicit, board members may assume or perceive that these behaviors are unwelcome; the Chair needs to encourage board members to speak up and affirm that conflicts are necessary (see Chapter 5).

This result is less surprising when we consider that the reasons to remain silent are on both conscious and unconscious levels. Here the "implicit voice" theory comes into place (Detert and Edmondson 2011). Implicit belief refers to our unconscious level and can be independent of the current environment. These beliefs are socially acquired and are implicit because we react subconsciously and automatically without consciously deciding to stay silent. The findings of Detert and Edmondson (2011) explain why managers are surprised to learn that individuals can be afraid to speak up, even if the environment supports a culture of speaking up. Since the reasons to remain silent are on both conscious and unconscious levels, it is unlikely that individuals will change their implicit behavior without being *continuously encouraged to speak up* (Bacharach, Bamberger, and McKinney 2000; Detert and Edmondson 2011).

Step 5/6: Show Vulnerability

Taking interpersonal risks is connected to the readiness to enter into conflicts and is also essential to build trust. If we look at Kets de Vries's (2011, p. 5) definition of the best team, he adds to taking risks and conflicts a further element—reciprocity in self-disclosure:

> The best team is one where members are ready to take personal risks, prepared to tackle conflict, and willing to have courageous conversations. However, these developments are contingent upon an underlying team culture of trust, reciprocity in self-disclosure to improve interpersonal dialogue and constructive conflict resolution.

Self-disclosure demands a lot of courage, the courage to be vulnerable. In adding another hot topic, "sharing vulnerability," to the chart, I recommend reading Brené Brown's *Dare to Lead* (2018). She claims that ego tries to minimize the feeling of being vulnerable because it is too risky. We ask ourselves, what will people think about me? Could I learn something unpleasant about myself? Brown (2018, p. 74) says:

> Ego is an eager and willing conspirator when it comes to locking away the heart; I think of my ego as my inner hustler. It is that voice in my head that drives pretending, performing, pleasing, and perfecting.

The ego craves acceptance and approval. It is about self-protection, not taking risks, but it closes down the heart. Brown (2018, p. 34) not only links taking risks and showing vulnerability, but also showing vulnerability and creating trust:

> We need to trust to be vulnerable, and we need to be vulnerable in order to build trust. Trust and vulnerability grow together and to betray one is to destroy both.

If your starting point is that you don't know if you can show vulnerability because you are not sure if you can trust the person, you may never know.

BM: You need to be prepared to show vulnerability because, with a facade, you are not building trust.

Figure 2.6 shows the connections between trust, feeling safe, taking risks, and showing vulnerability, indicating that those points depend on and reinforce each other.

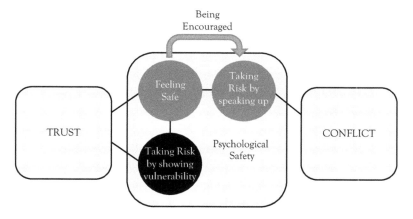

Figure 2.6 Show vulnerability

Without putting down our armor and shield, we will not learn—we will defend ourselves, hide our true feelings, and not connect! We should operate from "self-awareness and not self-protection," as Brown states. Showing vulnerability is not the norm in the business world:

BM: You can't show vulnerability. It is not accepted for a leader to show weaknesses.

Showing vulnerability in most cultures is believed to reveal extreme weakness of character, especially in a harsh business environment. But showing vulnerability is a strength, demonstrating courage and self-esteem.

BM: Vulnerability is very critical to me because it makes you remain authentic and not put up a show. You can be vulnerable and still be very strong. And being strong is needed because people want to be led by a real and humane leader who can inspire them.

By not hiding your feelings, you can build trust, connect with your true self, and establish better relationships. As social species, we are hard-wired for connections—without them, we suffer (see "belonging and attachment" later in this chapter).

I have always believed that vulnerability is a strength. But since showing emotions and vulnerability is so tenaciously considered as a weakness in our male-dominated business world, I include Brown's six myths of vulnerability:

1. *Vulnerability is weakness*—showing vulnerability takes courage.
2. *I don't do vulnerability*—you can consciously deal with your vulnerability and your emotions and how they affect your behavior, or you can let fear dominate your thinking and behavior. Pretending that we don't "do" vulnerability means that we are not aware that fear drives our behavior.
3. *I can go it alone*—we are hardwired for human connection.
4. *Engineer the uncertainty and discomfort out of vulnerability*—especially in technical industries, as I experienced in the insurance industry. Blocking out anxiety can lead to behavior that rationalizes; we need another expert opinion because we don't want to deal with anxiety. Displacing insecurity is not dealing with your fears.
5. *Trust comes before vulnerability*—trust and vulnerability go hand-in-hand, determining one another.
6. *Vulnerability is disclosure*—while leaders should create a safe space, it does not mean we should overshare; vulnerability needs boundaries.

After having conducted my interviews, I am convinced that developing a more relaxed attitude to vulnerability has massive potential for business relationships. I will return to this topic in the chapter about the relationship between the Chair and the Group CEO.

If we trust ourselves, we are more willing to take risks in self-disclosure or conflicts. We need trust and courage in addressing what we want. Addressing "what we want" can sound like a demand. Sharing a need is more profound. But what we should do is share a need with an explanation of why it is so vital: providing a frame, a context, for the other person. This requires deep-rooted self-esteem and/or courage, reinforcing the circle of building trust.

Step 6/6: Act, Reflect, and Learn

To manage the inevitable disagreements that arise when people work together, we have to develop interpersonal skills related to learning (*inquiry, curiosity, listening*) and teaching (*communicating, connecting, clarifying)* (Edmondson 2012). Kets de Vries (2011) calls such an environment a "coaching culture," one where people have interpersonal trust, are prepared for self-disclosure and openness to assess their strengths and weaknesses, and are willing to give clear and constructive feedback.

Edmondson (2012) uses "reflection" as her fourth ingredient for successful teaming instead of feedback. I have been a feedback fan for many years but am in the process of becoming an even bigger fan of reflection, to which I dedicate Part III of this book.

What may sound like common sense is far from common in the corporate world. "People who rarely experience failure, however, end up not knowing how to deal with it effectively. And this serves to reinforce the normal human tendency to reason defensively" (Argyris 1991, p. 8). Instead of suppressing doubts, we *should acknowledge emotions and reflect on* them publicly; then, we can learn and grow (Hirschhorn 1990; Edmondson and Smith 2006; Schön 2017).

The missing piece in the chart is step 6: a cloud of "act, reflect, and learn," which embraces all other points as shown in Figure 2.7.

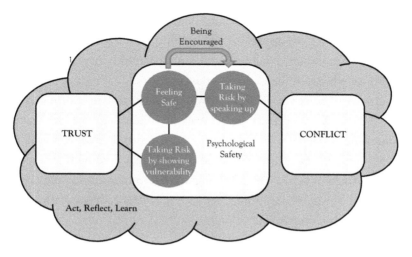

Figure 2.7 Act, reflect, and learn

We should learn how to develop trust, take a risk, talk about our needs, listen well, enter into conflicts, and heal wounds. And we should learn how to reflect together what we could do better in the future.

What Do Team Members Need to Flourish?

We have looked at what great teams do. In this section, I go one step deeper into what team members need to act as a great team.

If you have followed the previous chapter and are skillful, then maybe your team is already working well; team members feel safe, show vulnerability, enter into debates, and, above all, reflect together—the fundamental needs of your team members are satisfied. But being aware of each team's own needs that must be attended helps prevent crises or manage them better.

Board members may either have taken for granted that boards equipped with members who already had a successful career will automatically function well or did not care much about the impact the board had. To take the board's tasks and functions seriously, board members need time to spend together to develop as a team.

BM: What I feel in all groups or teams is, if you want intimacy within that group, you need to be prepared to spend some time together. As a management team, that is relatively easy to achieve; as a board team, you have to make an extra effort. But I have observed that the boards who make that effort develop a mutual interest and are more open and have fewer superficial conversations.

The short statements of board members' thinking given in the introduction, summarized in the chart in Figure 2.8, are expressions of feeling, sensing, or wishing, all having motive or reason.

Dysfunctional Board Behavior
- I am in. I want to get along. No reason to expose myself.
- I sense that the chair prefers not too many debates, and I act accordingly.
- It does not feel right if I speak up against the chair; it feels disloyal, I remain silent.
- I would like to make a difference and have an impact, but I am not sure how I can add value; so, let's be silent.
- I am used to having impact, and I will make a difference here. I tell management what to do!

Figure 2.8 Dysfunctional board behavior

If those needs, concerns, and fears are not satisfied or not contained, they may lead to dysfunctional behaviors.

It is not enough to put people together and expect them to work efficiently, even if they have a clear goal and sufficient resources. If you want to create a strong team, you as a leader should pay attention to the overt and covert forces underlying group life or, as Kets de Vries (2011) says, "there is much more to group interaction than meets the eye."

We are all, figuratively speaking, an iceberg: much more is happening below the surface than is shown above; there is more in our unconsciousness than in our consciousness.

The board of directors is called a "black box," but our brain was for a long time also a black box. We know today that our brain processes information consciously and unconsciously. According to Mlodinow (2013), our conscious mind can digest about 10 to 50 signals a second, while our brain receives more than 10 million signals. The unconscious mind is hyperactive and independent and plays a critical role in shaping how our conscious mind experiences and responds to the world. Consequently, our everyday behavior is influenced by factors we are not aware of.

This paradigm, called the psychodynamic approach, goes back to Freud's psychoanalytic theories (for an overview of the psychodynamic approach's young history, see Kets de Vries and Cheak 2014). To understand leadership behavior better, we have to explore those hidden undercurrents that affect human behavior. We tend to focus too firmly on rationality, structure, and processes but neglect the more emotional side (Zaleznik 1989). Therefore, I will touch briefly on some issues about our behavior in groups.

Belonging and Attachment

Belonging to a group where we feel recognized and understood is a strong human desire, essential for self-esteem. Applying this view to boards, it is evident that board members are less anxious about their work when they are part of a team that takes the time to build a sense of community and belonging. In the psychodynamic language, this need to belong is our "need for attachment," to be close with another human being. Applied to groups, this need can be described as *affiliation* (Kets de Vries 2011).

Human beings require both attachment to and separation from others to survive and regulate an interaction's intensity. Schopenhauer's parable of two hedgehogs illustrates our dilemma. If the hedgehogs try to warm each other and come too close, they prick each other; too distant, and they get cold. If we are securely attached, we have solid self-esteem and build relationships relatively quickly. Our attachment script affects our emotional management and will determine how we interact in a group setting (Kets de Vries 2011). Next is a short test about your attachment style.

Discover Your Attachment Style

Study the statements in Table 2.1 and label them TRUE or FALSE.

Table 2.1 Discover your attachment style

		TRUE	FALSE
1	It is relatively easy for me to become emotionally close to others. I am comfortable depending on others and having others depend on me.		
2	I want to be emotionally intimate with others, but I often find that others are reluctant to get as close as I would like.		
3	I am comfortable without close emotional relationships. It is very important to me to feel independent and self-sufficient, and I prefer not to depend on others or have others depend on me.		

If you select 1, you may be securely attached. If your answer is 2, you may fall into the anxious attachment group. If your answer is 3, you may be avoidant attached.

Source: Kets de Vries 2011

A different approach of relationship pattern style goes back to Thomann and Schulz von Thun (2003), who developed the Riemann/Thomann cross (Figure 2.9) with Riemann's recourse (1961). The model distinguishes between two opposing basic human orientations. On one axis are the terms "closeness" and "distance," on the other, "continuity" and "change."

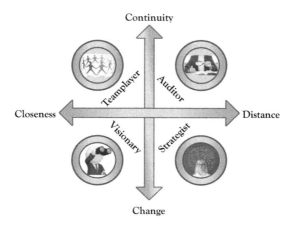

Figure 2.9 Riemann/Thomann model

These four basic orientations occur in different proportions in everyone. Someone can be further along on the distance axis than the one for closeness while standing in the middle on the continuity/change axis. For current well-being, usually only one or two orientations would be decisive. In stressful situations, needs become more apparent. The basic orientations have a direct influence on communication and relationship behavior. It is not easy to classify oneself since different priorities can be expressed in different situations despite the preference for a home area. I like to use the model in team coaching because it helps us understand ourselves and how we engage with others better.

Talking About Feelings, Concerns, Fear, and Even Shame

Being aware that we as board members also have needs as human beings, and remembering some earlier quotes from board members, it is clear that feelings—as concerns, fear, or even shame–affect our team behavior. Thoughts, feelings, impulses, and memories can be challenging to deal with. We apply an unconscious defense mechanism that puts distance between us and those unpleasant feelings to protect ourselves.

While this protects our ego from stress and anxiety, it avoids dealing with the real problem. Common defense mechanisms in the workplace include denial, projection, rationalization, or intellectualization (Cramer 2012). A typical example of rationalization is *I didn't get the job that I applied for, but I really didn't want it in the first place.* This attitude may make us feel better, and to that extent, is healthy, but it may mean a lack of curiosity as to the real reasons, and therefore not learning to do better in the future.

When the level of anxiety rises in an organization, executives typically rely on existing methods to solve problems: but rules, regulations, procedures, and organizational charts all offer insufficient containment for our emotional needs. They help us feel a false sense of security and control, leaving our emotions aside. Therefore, leaders have to offer possibilities for talking about fears and concerns or our defense reaction can turn dysfunctional (Krantz 2010; Kets de Vries and Cheak 2014).

Take the feeling of shame, for example. Shame is a powerful emotion, the one least often acknowledged in the workplace: it is hard to recognize and, once identified, painful to address (Brown 2018). It can be described as a fear of disconnection because we are flawed (Brown 2018). Shame is feeling bad about the *"self"*—*I am bad*—compared to guilt, where I did something bad. Shame goes deeper and is an attack on ourselves (Kets de Vries 2011).

Healthy humans all experience shame sometimes. But when preoccupied with feelings of shame, we protect ourselves and do not open up. As we have seen, openness and self-disclosure are essential for teams: shame is a killer for a trusted relationship. Shame and a low sense of self-esteem are intimately related as both are associated with negative self-perception. The less we can talk about shame, the more control it has over our lives (Brown 2018). What follows is a brief test about feelings of shame.

Are you haunted by feelings of shame or guilt?

Label the statements in Table 2.2 TRUE or FALSE.

Table 2.2 Are you haunted by feelings of shame or guilt?

		TRUE	FALSE
1	I constantly think about past failures or experiences of rejection.		
2	I have always had a sense of inferiority.		
3	I am generally disgusted with myself.		
4	I have never liked the way I look.		
5	I am extremely sensitive to criticism.		
6	When criticized, I tend to blame others.		
7	I am very anxious in public situations.		
8	I am considered shy.		
9	I have always doubted myself.		

If most of these statements are TRUE, you are prone to strong feelings of SHAME. You are very critical of yourself. You have a constant fear of rejection.
Source: Kets de Vries 2011

We must let those emotions emerge and be identified, and deal with them. Leaders need to create a safe space environment where our inner world, like fears and concerns, can be shared, which—if done rightly—"helps create a virtuous circle of trust, self-disclosure, empathy, and acceptance" (Kets de Vries 2011).

In the previous section, we looked at our basic needs in teams. If we belong to a team, feel safe, and address what is bothering us, we can act in a way that brings the best out of us. It is not enough to have a common purpose and enough resources. We should look at what the team and each individuum need to work at their best. Great teams are engaged, show passion for their task, are ready to tackle difficult issues, do not shy away from conflict, and have strong bonds.

Research has shown that the simple awareness of boards' psychosocial processes helps board members' interactions (Schroeder and Prentice 1998). Boards have to create awareness of the invisible issues affecting those interactions: they have to be aware that they are a team where the overall setup does not favor open dialogue. Boards should take their time to work not only on content but also to form a team. Individual needs may be very different:

BM: I feel lonely on the board because I am not feeling connected to the other board members and I also don't know what is expected from me.

BM: I belonged to a board, but I did not want to belong to their social club. I wasn't "clubbable." I was the only real independent thinker who was lonely, and I went through a lot of anxiety about what to do and not to do.

While both board members feel lonely in the previous statements, one would like to feel a stronger bonding, and the other is afraid of losing his independence. Which degree of "closeness" is the right one is not for me to judge, but I do believe that by not talking about these feelings, they are hindering the development of a team where members work at their best. According to Kegan, Lahey, Fleming and Miller (2014), the effort we put in to preserve our reputations and hide our true feelings and inadequacies from others is "the single biggest cause of wasted resources in nearly every company today."

As Kegan et al. (2014, p. 46) put it:

Ordinarily, in an effort to protect ourselves, we allow gaps to form—between plans and actions, between ourselves and others, between who we are at work and our "real selves," between what we say at the coffee machine and what we say in the meeting room. These gaps are most often created by the conversations we are not having, the synchronicities with others we're not achieving, and the work that, out of self-protection, we're avoiding.

Organizations and their teams—in board teams, as in any other team—must create a trustworthy and reliable environment where members feel safe to expose themselves in order to grow as individuals and as a team.

That closes the circle of this chapter and leads to the person in the best position to create such a safe space: the Chair. A Chair who sticks to the essence of this quote:

BM: Rather have no team than a team of yes men.

CHAPTER 3

The Role of the Chair

The most difficult thing is to know yourself.

—Thales

It is of practical value to learn to like yourself. Since you must spend so much time with yourself, you might as well get some satisfaction out of the relationship.

—Norman Vincent Peale

The Chair's Multifaceted Role

The official role of the Chair is, in general, well understood. He has to ensure, with his board, that the company has the right strategy, adequate governance and control structure, a good culture, and the right people in place and in the pipeline. The Chair and his board try to ensure that the CEO and the management team are successful and take a long-term view.

The less-discussed role of the Chair is relational. The Chair should be able and willing to form an excellent board team, and the Chair should be able to manage a productive relationship with the management, particularly with the CEO.

The Chair should also cultivate good relations outside the company. Investors want to talk with the Chair about strategy, culture, and governance, quite correctly, a task that has grown in recent years. The media also likes a piece of his attention. Especially in a highly regulated business, the regulator plays an important role that needs to be fostered. Being in touch with relevant political figures and legislators is not to be underestimated for its long-term benefits.

Chairs do well to remember that building trustful relationship needs time and attention. It is not enough to get in touch with people when you need them. Typically, company representatives—like the Chair—have a significant content advantage when dealing with political figures. It is only natural that the person who has less specific knowledge will react with a degree of mistrust; it helps nurture those relationships and to be considered a reasonable person who can think more broadly than just your business interests.

Building a network of resilient relationships with different shareholders and stakeholders is vital for a Chair. Other board members can certainly support him, but he remains the primary person to build and nurture those very different relationships, each calling for different strengths. Without diminishing these external relationships, I will focus on the interactions within the company.

Being the Chair is a multifaceted position. The Chair position is powerful, one from which you *can* do a lot: in fact, much more than you actually *should* do. Finding the balance of using this power for the company's benefit rather than strengthening your position can be challenging and demands considerable self-awareness. Once you are elected to a powerful position, learning and developing do not become any more comfortable.

Based on my interviews and experience, I will summarize the Chair's essential personality traits in this chapter. The corporate world rightfully allows a variety of suitable solutions, and by no means do I favor a rigid description of the ideal profile. Nevertheless, I will point out some general remarks that don't always get the necessary attention. I focus—in line with Shekshnia and Zagieva (2019)—on *soft skills*. They state that the job of "a Chair is almost exclusively about human relations" calling upon diverse roles and backgrounds. Exceptional behavioral skills are required.

BM: A Chair must like people.

BM: When you look at how boards work, you often get people promoted to boards or Chairs because they've had a successful career but haven't necessarily understood the mechanisms of the human element to run a board. Managing a board and interacting with the management team needs a very different skillset, often underestimated.

Focusing on the behavioral skills of the Chair should not exclude the organization. Depending on the organization's history and understanding of the Chair's role, the focus on which skills are of utmost importance will differ.

Person/Role/System

A person fills a role, but—in the case of a Chair—the role is accompanied by a significant organizational context and often a long history. Organizatisonal role analysis shows that any role sits at the intersection of the system and the person, as shown in Figure 3.1.

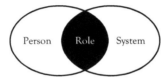

Figure 3.1 Organizational role analysis

Although a role is a structural part of the system, it is filled and shaped by the incumbent and influenced by predecessors. Anyone brings their experiences in different roles in business and their private life to their role. Each person brings their particular understanding to new roles. An organization is also heavily influenced by understanding the role in the context of the past, of images of predecessors. There are endless interactions, connections, influences, and interdependencies between the organization, the role, and the person (Long 2018).

Our own experiences bias our expectations of what the Chair's role is. Suppose you are about to hire a Chair or other top senior executive or coach such a person. You would be well advised to conduct an organizational role analysis to have a closer look at the overall system, the role, and the personality. A new appointment is the chance to reevaluate. You may, in the end, decide to continue with the role as it currently stands, but the exercise is nevertheless helpful because, as an organization, you have made a conscious choice. Or perhaps you decide that it is time to adapt the definition of the role. Whether or not the board favors to adapt the role at the end, your exercise will sharpen the profile focus in searching for a new Chair. I encourage you to look at the bigger picture and not assume that continuing as you always have done is the right thing to do or, simply because of bad experiences, doing the opposite.

Addressing those questions while hiring a new CEO is more common than hiring a new Chair. Hiring a new CEO, the Chair and a nomination committee are typically in charge. Hiring a new Chair, you usually have the incumbent in place; any questions about a different understanding of the future role can be considered criticism of the "old" Chair. I stress this point, knowing that board members like to shy away from those areas of potential conflicts. While the incumbent will undoubtedly add to this picture, he should not be at the frontline of the process. Companies with an independent lead director may be better equipped to deal with those succession questions.

Subsequently, it is essential to communicate the expectations for the role to align perceptions and reality for those in touch with the Chair, primarily internally. Old habits and expectations of the role are woven into a company's cultural DNA, and conscious and repetitive awareness is needed to change the understanding of the role.

I include these comments not out of a fascination for the powerful concept of organizational role analysis but to be explicit that filling a role needs to consider the organization *and* the person.

Hiring a new Chair requires context. In my attempt to develop essential personality traits for a Chair, I lack a concrete organization, the history of the role as understood within a particular organization, and its regulatory framework and legal environment. Rather, I will paint a picture of the personality traits of an ideal Chair without the benefit of a concrete situation. That said, the interviews in more than 20 different countries showed a relatively coherent picture of what is needed in a formidable Chair. Depending on the situation, you will weigh some traits more heavily than others.

Moderator Versus Expert

Since many interviewees addressed whether the Chair should be a moderator or an expert, I will put that question front and center.

BM: My experience shows that Chairs often misinterpret their role. They think they have to be leaders in content. The Chair should not feel responsible for leading on substance. Heaven knows that the body of the board is always good enough to deal with substantive issues.

BM: The Chair is like a conductor, getting the voices from all the players and letting the "soloist" know that now it is not his moment to play. The moderating role of the Chair is the most important and the least mastered.

BM: The Chair's ability to moderate is vital to unlocking the board's potential power.

BM: There is no need for the Chair to be the expert, but he must be a top moderator.

These quotes represent the prevailing view about the Chair's role: *less as a content expert—more of an orchestrating role, a moderator.* Acknowledging that role and walking the talk can be different sides of the coin.

BM: As a Chair, you have a content advantage compared to the other board members; and you are also in charge of getting the meeting done in the expected timeframe. It is not easy to decide where to let a discussion float and where you are more directive, especially if you believe the direction is clear.

BM: Sometimes, you just want to demonstrate that you are prepared and that you know the issues and then you may fall into the trap of showing off.

The interviewees mentioned several reasons why the qualities of the moderator do not play a more prominent role in selecting Chairs. Chairs are sometimes chosen out for the "wrong" reasons (relationship issues, public reputation); the awareness that those more psychological qualities are crucial is not mainstream. The capital market and the media can't assess these less overt qualities but can determine expertise, so the outside world's perception can play too significant a role.

BM: Nobody dares appoint someone as Chair simply because of his personality; if he doesn't have a lot to show in this field of expertise, the choice is limited. We are looking for so-called experts in this kind of defined skills and expertise, which we almost have to prove today; we are bringing something to the fore that we can prove. Simultaneously, the moderating personality, the leadership qualities, cannot be commented on by the public and commentators and therefore doesn't focus on it.

Having established that the moderator role is essential but may not have gained its rightful place, what about the expertise of a Chair? If we look for expertise, who has more expertise than a former CEO? Former CEOs are often Chairs later in their career. While having the experience of leading a company and knowing the business seems to be a significant advantage, it bears certain risks. A Chair's role is quite different from that of the CEO.

BM: You can't start messing with the management; you can question them, you can give tips, and you can disagree, but you can't make the mistake of actually telling them how to do their job. That is delegated, and you have to respect that. In my experience, former CEOs have the most significant challenge here.

As a common-sense rule, some industry knowledge seems to be of advantage. However, Shekshnia (2018) states that the majority in his study felt that it might even be a handicap to be an expert since experts tend to find solutions on their own rather than organizing a collective decision-making process. The following quote expresses a balanced view:

BM: The Chair should do very little talking himself but motivate others to join in; the board members realize that their input is essential. He needs to be 100 percent moderator of a team. He must know the subject matter, but he doesn't have to be a specialist. In our company, it is clear that the Chair comes from a different industry. How to make the group come alive, that is the most important thing.

I favor specific industry knowledge, especially in technically complex industries like financial services. But maybe this is typical insider bias.

While the moderator role was undisputed, some CEOs expressed their preference for a Chair with industry-specific knowledge.

> *BM: I want to have a strong sparring partner whom I can meet on eye level. I want to be transparent and intellectually honest. If he doesn't know the business, then it will be difficult.*

> *BM: The Chair needs to have a lot of subject matter expertise; he needs to be very competent; then you can discuss important issues and have proper conversations.*

> *BM: I want to have a very strong, competent Chair in my business. I have benefited a lot, honestly, from different points of view. Because otherwise, you are just a lonely guy, pretending to know everything or thinking you know everything.*

> *BM: The Chair needs to be strong, well connected in the specific business, ready to go deep if necessary, and know the business. If not, the CEO will lead the board.*

I liked the attitude of these CEOs because it expresses the need for a content exchange with the Chair rather than a perspective of power and control. Overall, I found it remarkable that the role of a Chair acting as a moderator and forming a team received so much weight in the interviews, while the question of being an expert got very polarized views. With (hopefully) more diverse, independent, and active boards in the future (see Chapters 2 and 5), the moderator role will be even more critical. One Chair stated:

> *BM: My biggest challenge as a Chair in managing the interactions between board members—having some exciting personalities on the board—is to conclude without voting at every board meeting.*

Obviously, if you want to have an active board with real debates, moderator qualities are essential. Being a good moderator goes hand-in-hand with a dynamic team.

> *BM: In a board, you have mainly "alpha animals"; my job is to form a team and not just to have a bunch of individuals sitting around a table.*

The moderator role is closely linked with the capability of developing and relying on a team, while the expert has less need for a team since the Chair with the CEO already has the answers. As a passive board member, you may prefer the Chair's expertise because it is more comfortable to rely on expert opinion.

If the Chair is an industry expert, it is even more critical to understand his personality. Does he define himself as an expert? Can you determine whether he is leaning toward acting as an expert from his work history and personality? One former CEO (and now Chair) stated:

> BM: A CEO needs to have somebody who says: "No, yes, but or pay attention." However, the more the Chair knows, the more he has to restrain himself from displaying an attitude—I know that. I am the expert. Ultimately, the Chair has to leave the CEO to do his job and not interfere too much.

I will come back to that specific challenge in Chapter 6 when I address the Chair–CEO relationship, but the quote leads to the next section: what personality traits a Chair should possess.

The Essential Personality Traits for a Chair

The moderator skills had more weight than the need to be an expert in the interviews. Moderator skills are also closer to my list of essential personality traits for a Chair. Skills may express the technical capabilities, while personality leans more toward whether a person can apply the skills in critical moments.

> BM: If the personality is not right, then the best skills are not much use.

As a tennis player, you may have an excellent serve, but perhaps in the decisive moment, you can't demonstrate it. And a Chair will face many such critical situations, where he needs to react immediately and some-times lead others to a decision that may be unpopular. Based on my inter-views and my experience, some personal qualities that I believe to be vital for a Chair are listed in Figure 3.2.

Chair's Personality Traits
- High ethical standards, values-driven
- Self-esteem and being humble
- Self-aware and reflective
- Managing relationships
- Authenticity paired with flexibility and empathy
- Say "yes" to tension and conflict
- Having good judgment
- Summarizing and framing

Figure 3.2 Chair's personality traits

High Ethical Standards, Values-Driven

According to an international study by Giles (2016), high ethical and moral standards were the most critical leadership competencies out of a list of 74 items. Values-based leaders provide a safe and trusting environment where employees focus on productive social engagement, innovation, creativity, and ambition. As Giles (2016, p. 3) describes:

> Neuroscience corroborates this point. When the amygdala registers a threat to our safety, arteries harden and thicken to handle an increased blood flow to our limbs in preparation for a fight-or-flight response. In this state, we lose access to the limbic brain's social engagement system and the executive function of the prefrontal cortex, inhibiting creativity and the drive for excellence. From a neuroscience perspective, making sure that people feel safe on a deep level should be job number1 for leaders.

Leaders who have clear values and act consistently—especially in the so-called "moments of truth"—instill a sense of safety and trust, and people feel they can be relied on. The CEO and management must rely on the Chair; otherwise, it is hard to instill a culture of trust and psychological safety within the management team and the workforce.

High ethical standards and values-driven behavior provide an orientation for our daily business environment and decisions that are not always so straightforward as in textbooks.

Many years ago, we introduced a "dilemma game" at my former employer. We described a dilemma on the front of cards; on the back were different answers with different points. The goal was to get as many points as possible. However, the overall objectives were that teams discuss their solution and compare it with the preferred solution from the employer's perspective. Compliance, especially in the financial sector, develops into a checkbox mindset. Independently of how many rules and regulations we produce, we will always face situations where there is no clear and convincing "black-and-white answer." If we already face such a dilemma in compliance, where standard procedures need to be applied in the same way by many different people, how often do the Chair and CEO face such conflicting situations?

If the company has behavioral values where management walks the talk, such values-based behavior increases the psychological safety of both management and employees, and therefore the decision-making process.

Management needs to know that the Chair will not sacrifice his values for short-term gain. As tempting it may be, the price to be paid for bending your values goes well beyond the risk of getting caught: you instill insecurity in the workplace. A classic example is how the company deals with situations with a commercial impact that call for an ethical response, for example, successful salespeople who violate the company's espoused values. As tempting, it may be to look away, don't.

To know that the Chair adheres to ethical values and is unwilling to compromise them is the necessary foundation for the company. It provides guidance and safety for all involved. I will come back to specific values in the next subchapters, which I believe to be particularly important for Chairs.

Self-Esteem and Being Humble

According to James (1890), self-esteem is a product of "perceived competence in domains of importance." So, self-esteem stems from the belief that we are good at things that matter to us. Does self-esteem support or hinder our relationship capabilities?

My personal experience is that I got along better with people—especially those further up the hierarchy—who I believed had solid self-esteem. Especially in my younger years, I could be a challenge for authority, particularly in military service. Superiors who felt secure could handle me better. Often, I was proud that I spoke up and challenged bosses. I had a long way to go in learning how to challenge people. I am still learning, but age has made me a little less direct and more subtle. I discussed and reflected upon those topics early on, and my conclusion was clear: people with solid self-esteem can handle a behavior where people speak up or a controversial situation much better. If you have high self-esteem, it is easier to accept criticism. You don't take it so personally.

> *BM: People soon realized that I have enough self-esteem to take criticism or contradiction, which has a contagious quality.*

> *BM: High self-esteem is essential for Chair; you have to trust yourself to trust others, and you are more likely to be ready for conflict and live with uncertainty.*

So, I was happy to read—decades later in the *Harvard Business Review*—that "people acting in an abusive arrogant or demeaning manner to others their behavior almost always is a symptom of their lack of self-esteem. They need to put someone else down to feel good about themselves" (Christensen, in Drucker 2010).

Having solid self-esteem provides you with the inner security that you don't need to avoid all tension. It causes you to be less shy about avoiding conflict because conflict does not lead you to question yourself. As Amy Edmondson (2012) states: "You can't have serious work without conflict." As we have seen, being open to conflict is necessary for a successful team. It is so crucial for a Chair that I will come back to it in a separate subsection.

So, high self-esteem helps persevere tension. But does high self-esteem not lead to an inflated ego with all its downsides? A former CEO—now board member—articulates her biggest nightmare as CEO:

> *BM: A big ego in the Chair and then a weak board is the horror for a CEO.*

Does high self-esteem equal big ego?

BM: People often think that high self-esteem has to do with a big ego. I don't think so. It's just nonegoistic self-esteem. It must be in the sense that my personality value is not measured by whether I am always right, but a quiet—inner—security; even if I am wrong, I am me. No jagged edge falls out of my crown when I make a mistake. This is almost essential for good leadership.

BM: The Chair needs self-esteem that comes from within and is not dependent on public applause; he also requires humility. One must be prepared to be questioned as a person and not feel that this is a crime against creation.

I realized in my interviews that we often have very different understandings of self-esteem. With self-esteem, the ego can move more to the background; you are assured that you are grounded, centered, and balanced.

Christensen (in Drucker 2010) writes that high self-esteem goes hand-in-hand with being humble. You can be humble only if you feel good about yourself, but it is neither an inflated ego nor a lack of self-esteem. To quote the Irish author C.S. Lewis: "Humility isn't thinking less of yourself, but thinking of yourself less." High self-esteem allows you to not search for center stage. You are comfortable in your skin and place in life (Charan, Carey, and Useem 2012). You need less constant admiration, which is an excellent attitude for the role of a Chair, who should be not too dominating a force (see Chapter 6). Often, the need to "toot your own horn" compensates for a lack of confidence.

If you are courageous, I suggest that you and your partner or somebody from your business environment fill in the short questionnaire (Table 3.1) about being humble and reflect upon your respective views.

Being humble should not be confused with being soft. Humble people can be firm and clear in tense personal situations. They are people with principles who put principles before the self. The opposite of humility is putting the ego above the principle (Covey and Merrill 2006).

Being humble also helps you to listen. Listening to different perspectives is an essential skill for a Chair. I will come back to this vital quality in the chapter about the Chair–CEO's relationship.

Table 3.1 How humble are you in a leadership role?

Indicate your humbleness in a leadership role by choosing how strongly you agree with the questions below on a scale from 1 (strongly disagree) to 5 (strongly agree). Then consider giving the (uncompleted) questionnaire to your partner, boss or direct report.

		strongly disagree 1	2	3	4	strongly agree 5
1	I seek out feedback, even if it's critical.					
2	If I don't know how to do something, I am comfortable in admitting it.					
3	I willingly acknowledge where others are more knowledgeable or skilled than I am.					
4	I look for others' skills and positive contributions.					
5	I take time to compliment others on what they do well.					
6	I make sure that others know I appreciate their contributions.					
7	I know that I can learn from others and am open to doing so.					
8	I am open to ideas and advice from others.					

Source: Adapted from Mayo 2018 with reference to Bradley Owens

If you have high self-esteem, you are more grounded and less driven by fear. Fear narrows perceptions and awareness of others. You can be distracted by anxiety and struggle to sense what is going on around you. Being self-aware and sensing others, the topic of the following subchapters is crucial for a Chair.

Self-Aware and Reflective

According to Kets de Vries (2006), leaders often have a public self that they share and a private one that is not shared; the nonshared self can appear quite different from the public one. Sometimes leaders do not know that self in any depth. Leaders don't necessarily understand why they do what they do: much is below conscious awareness. Past successes, inherent time pressure, and prestigious position do not support self-reflective behavior.

Leaders are surrounded by liars, says Kets de Vries (2006). They have to recognize that people who report to them sugarcoat situations, either consciously for political reasons or unconsciously as a transferential reaction. "Leaders need to continually ask themselves whether their own mirror hunger is encouraging dishonesty in the ranks" (Kets de Vries 2006). The higher you ascend the corporate ladder, the more challenging it is to get candid feedback; without—it is hard to learn to adjust, and you run the risk of making mistakes that damage your organization and your reputation.

Kaplan (in Drucker 2010) suggests that you should look to yourself for answers. Asking the right questions is far more important than having all the answers. You have to have a reflective mind to get to know yourself. In one of the most successful business books ever written, *The 7 Habits of Highly Effective People*, Stephen Covey (2020) favors an "inside-out" approach, starting first with the self: your paradigms, character, and motives. In the Executive Master program for Coaching and Consulting for Change at INSEAD, we often heard from our professors, Erik van de Loo and Roger Lehman, that we should use ourselves as a tool.

Peter Drucker says that you have to be your own CEO because companies do not manage their knowledge workers' careers. If you want to be consistently productive, you have to have a deep understanding of yourself. What are your most valuable strengths? What are your most dangerous weaknesses? The implication for Drucker (2010) is clear: "Only when you operate from a combination of your strengths and self-knowledge can you achieve true—and lasting—excellence."

So, you should regularly take your time and reflect upon questions like:

- What are my values?
- What are my strengths?

- Who am I?
- Where do I belong?
- How do I act under pressure?

According to Goleman, Boyatzis, and McKee (2001, p. 49): "Self-awareness, perhaps the most essential of the emotional intelligence competencies, is the ability to read your own emotions. It allows people to know their strengths and limitations and feel confident about their self-worth."

While being reflective is vital for all leaders, it is crucial for the Chair because the role has many layers and calls for a broad repertoire of actions and reactions. Or as William George (Goleman, Langer, Congleton, and McKee 2017, p. 15) puts it:

Authentic leadership begins with self-awareness or knowing yourself deeply. Self-awareness is not a trait you are born with but the capacity you develop throughout your lifetime. It's your understanding of your strengths and weaknesses, your purpose in life, your values and motivations, and how and why you respond to situations in a particular way. It requires a great deal of introspection and the ability to internalize feedback from others.

Here are some beautifully self-reflective statements from Chairs:

BM: I think my biggest challenge as a Chair is not to be the first but the last person speaking; I should not feel frustrated that everybody already said what I intended to say. It is a fight with my ego. I know that a different perspective is that I should be proud of the team and feel aligned with my team that my points were already brought up.

BM: He is bullying me. In the end, I can't control how another person reacts, but I can control how I react.

BM: As a Chair, I entered a board that was not very professional. The CEO was great with our customers but had trouble making decisions and was not interested in finance and regulatory stuff. Finance and Compliance started almost to report to me. I practically became *an executive chair, but I realized that was dangerous because I was subverting and marginalizing the CEO. I talked with him, offering advice and training, but it did not get better. The board was pleased with my extended role, and honestly, I was happy too. I love to work, and I have the capacity. We talked on the board about the shortcomings of the CEO, but we didn't fire him. I was much too tolerant of his performance and behavior. It needed a particular trigger for us to finally let the CEO go. We told ourselves that we wanted to be fair and human to the CEO, but honestly, I enjoyed my de facto "CEO" role with today's lenses. In a way, I was frustrated by not being the CEO.*

A well-known matrix in management circles is the Johari window (Figure 3.3), which puts the challenge of self-knowledge in quadrants. Self-disclosure helps to become more transparent and build trust (see earlier in Chapter 2).

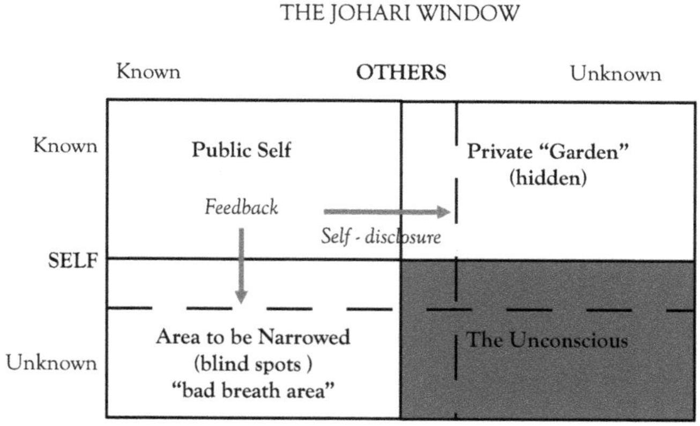

THE JOHARI WINDOW

Figure 3.3 Johari window

Discovering the unconscious can be a treasure but often needs great effort. Our blind spots, known to others but not to ourselves, can be easily accessed by honest feedback. Feedback may hurt and need time to digest, but it increases our self-knowledge of how we come across others. And it helps us to manage relationships. According to Covey (2020): "Anytime I have a relationship problem, my experience is that four out of five times, it's me, not them, and the key to fixing the problem is getting myself right first."

As much as I advocate being self-aware, I end with a note of caution; as with many things in life, it is a question of finding the right balance. Too much self-awareness can, according to Professor John D. Mayer (Goleman et al. 2017), actually harm self-esteem.

Managing Relationships

If we follow Goleman et al. (2001) regarding emotional intelligence, self-awareness is the starting point—followed by:

- Self-management
- Social awareness
- Relationship management

Knowing yourself better makes it easier to manage and control emotions; you can better explain the emotions or reactions, making you a more reliable and trustworthy partner. Knowing your emotions and feelings helps you also recognize others' emotions better.

> BM: I am more comfortable in my skin because I know what I know, and I know what I don't know. If I don't know something, I am more willing to ask for help. To reach that state has been a journey of self-awareness that helped me understand myself better as a person and the importance of a support system.

Being calmer and more relaxed within yourself means that you need less energy for self-management and gives you space to sense others' emotions. Allowing more debates in the board room means it is essential to have a heightened sense of what is going on (social awareness) using intuition and empathy. Those capabilities will enable you to manage relationships if you are willing to act upon them, which means that you are not just aware of what's going on but can address delicate topics. Communication skills are essential. You need the capability to bond, communicate clearly and convincingly, and disarm conflicts.

"Emotional leadership isn't just putting on a game face every day. It means understanding your impact on others—then adjusting your style accordingly." The good news is that emotional intelligence can be learned at any age. Still, you need motivation, willingness, and input from honest people (Goleman et al. 2001).

Authenticity Paired With Flexibility and Empathy

For me, authenticity is a crucial value. Without authenticity, it is hard to develop trusting relationships.

The word "authenticity" has its roots in the Greek term *authentes*, being true to oneself. You can't be authentic to yourself if you can't be true to others. I refer to a beautiful book by Margarita Mayo, *Yours Truly* (2018). She distinguishes three parts of authentic leadership:

- Heart (emotional authenticity—look inside yourself and find passion)
- Habit (behavioral authenticity—seek out honest feedback and develop a growth mindset)
- Harmony (social authenticity—seek a harmonious unity between yourself and others)

Authenticity is the essence of human well-being. When we feel consistency with our values, we feel a positive emotion—authenticity. Being authentic has strong links to self-esteem, knowing yourself, and being reflective because "being authentic" needs the relational link to somebody else. People who feel authentic report having higher gratitude and more self-esteem, which, as we saw earlier, is essential for a Chair (Mayo 2018, p. 15 with reference to a study by Lyubomirsky and Lepper 1999).

One should not limit authenticity to your own dictates; otherwise, we are heading toward narcissism (see the digression in Chapter 6); we should try to be true to ourselves in relation to others (harmony). Authenticity is not naked honesty. It has to fit the social circumstances; in German, the word *stimmig* translates (poorly) as coherent and harmonious. For example, if somebody asks when you are in a group, "Who do you dislike most?" it is not an authentic behavior to say so-and-so because it is not *stimmig*.

To seek harmony, we need to be aware of ourselves and others. We should develop a growth mindset habit—personal growth is a critical element of a person's psychological well-being. Feedback helps us check differing perceptions.

An accurate assessment of authenticity comes from evaluating the gap between our perception and third-party feedback; typically, we perceive ourselves better than our colleagues. Psychologists call this "motivated reasoning"; supposedly, it is healthy. "Motivated reasoning" helps us believe in our competence and allows us to see ourselves in a positive light. A million high school seniors were asked about their ability to get along with others: 60 percent rated themselves in the top 10 percent, and 25 percent rated themselves in the top 1 percent (College Board 1976). We are blessed with a talent to justify our rosy image of ourselves using credible arguments (Mlodinow 2013).

Can we overstress authenticity? According to Ibarra (2015), authenticity is overrated. Too strong a sense of who we are can lead to a recipe for staying stuck in the past. Being a chameleon can be advantageous because we adapt to the demands of the situation. One of Ibarra's slightly provocative subtitles reads: "Why feeling like a fake can be a sign of growth." As a firm believer in authenticity, her statement was difficult to digest but triggered some reflections. Mayo (2018) addresses it more subtly. Her book aims to resolve the growth authenticity paradox: How to balance one's behavioral integrity and growth? Mayo's book is about how to learn, grow, and stay authentic at the same time. Mayo champions an attitude of modifying our reactions by the situation's needs: political savvy does not make you less authentic. Practice behavioral flexibility, and you are still authentic.

BM: Learning to acknowledge another person's viewpoint, independent of its relevance, helped me develop a better working relationship and be more efficient.

Knowing your strength and balancing it is almost an art. In the digression on the next two pages (Figure 3.4), I introduce a concept which deals with the challenge of balancing our strengths.

As the personal example shows in Figure 3.4, learning to stay authentic and flexible at the same time can be challenging. I learned something else. I could speak up to a superior and be authentic; by doing so, I was courageous and stuck to my values, which meant that I could be satisfied with myself. Using Mayo's terminology, that is the "heart" part. I felt good—but I may have neglected the other person's feelings. I was not empathetic. Stein and Book (2011, p. 13) describe empathy: "It is the

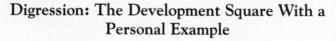

Digression: The Development Square With a Personal Example

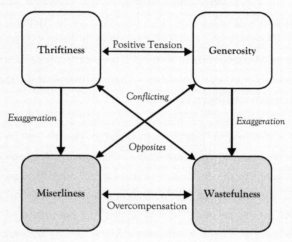

Figure 3.4 Value quadrant

Each person has some core qualities. If you start with one of them (like thriftiness) and go into overdrive, this quality or strength can turn into a weakness that derails them. If you want to improve a weakness, you should strive for the opposite "sister virtue" of the primary strength. The concept is called the development square or value quadrant (Schulz von Thun 1999 based on Helwig 1967). The value quadrant offers the opportunity to talk about a virtue and its exaggeration. It avoids a black-and-white view because the boundaries are fluid. It is an excellent tool for mediating conflict situations as well as self-reflection. It is much easier to accept working on not overstressing a strength than working on a weakness. If your spouse tells you that she loves your generosity, but sometimes it is too much, you hear it differently than if she were to say that you are "a wastrel."

If you do a value quadrant for yourself, I suggest you start with a personal strength (top left corner) and then search for the appropriate word to be used if you overdo that strength. Look for the sister virtue, which might show you your development areas (top right corner) and finish with the lower right corner.

I wrote my thesis (Sieber 2019a) about speaking up because it is vital to my personality. It has to do with a value that is very important to me: *authenticity*. If I overdo authenticity, I can come across as stubborn or rigid (Figure 3.5).

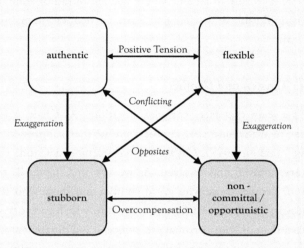

Figure 3.5 Picture of my authenticity value quadrant

The value quadrant in Figure 3.5 helped me to talk about a typical conflict pattern with a colleague. While I was more on the left, I perceived my peer on the right side. Which side is better is not the issue: you need both virtues, depending on the situation. Still, instead of blaming the other for a "weakness," the mutual recognition of a strength has helped our relationship and conflict behavior.

ability to non-judgmentally put into words your understanding of the other person's perspective on the world, even if you don't agree with it, or even if you find that perspective ridiculous." Howard Book taught me at the EMC at INSEAD to use empathy when you don't feel like it. As long as you stick to your core values, you cannot betray your authenticity by being empathetic.

A Chair's task requires *strong authenticity, with functional flexibility and empathy at the same time.* With the moderator role of the Chair in mind, a more guarded or self-effacing reaction may be, in general, more appropriate but challenging in your quest for authenticity.

New roles demand that our behavioral repertoire grows with new challenges. Evolving is only possible if we are willing to try out things without feeling that we are betraying ourselves. Without self-awareness and third-party input, it is hard to find the right balance in your competence, especially in an area where you are proud of your strength. Despite being flexible and willing to learn, authenticity remains crucial for any Chair.

Say Yes to Tension and Conflict

A board is a team that faces complex situations. As Chair, it is one of your tasks "to make sure that conflicts are neither suppressed nor circumvented" (Schön 2017). Organizational learning demands that such conflicts are surfaced and resolved. As we saw in Chapter 2, there are two types of people: those who avoid conflict and those who seek conflict. Especially as Chair, you should know into which category you fall. But, independent of your personal preference, it is a different story if two people for whom you are responsible (parent to child, superior to direct reports) have a heated debate. It feels uncomfortable. And that is the situation a Chair will face when encouraging debate.

According to Lencioni (2002), one of the most attractive traps to fall into is prematurely interrupting a discussion to protect members from harm. Participants will not learn conflict management skills, and a lack of resolution leaves them exposed. Being aware of that trap and your conflict tendency allows you to overrule your default:

BM: We must be aware of how we usually react in conflicts and learn to accept conflicts; I don't like conflict; to be honest, I hate it, but sometimes, it is just necessary.

BM: With my Chair, the sparks already fly; we are both strong personalities with strong opinions, but we are not vindictive; it is essential that things get on the table. There is nothing worse than when problems just ferment away.

BM: Conflicts weigh on me a lot. It's best to address the conflicts openly, but I don't always have that strength.

Saying yes to tensions means encouraging others to address issues, intervening if necessary.

> *BM: We deliberately say "yes" to conflicts. Conflicts are not harmful to me. I even love conflicts. Conflicts create friction, and friction creates heat. I consciously show appreciation for the one who has stood up for an opinion and then is defeated. As a Chair, you also have to endure not getting away with your opinion. It is not about you, it is about your function, and your function serves your team and the company's well-being. However, heated debates have to be conducted well by the Chair; most importantly, you have to go for a beer afterward.*

We all know that a single dissenter can make a huge difference. Therefore, it is crucial that the Chair explicitly and sincerely praises them. *Dissent is not disloyalty.* Feeling an obligation of loyalty to the Chair is a common motive for silence for board members (Sieber 2019a). A Chair needs to combine emotional intelligence and the courage to welcome tough questions. He has to act as a role model and challenge himself by saying "yes" to conflict. As Ronald Heifetz (Goleman et al. 2017) writes: "It demands a commitment to serve others; skill at diagnostic, strategic, and tactical reasoning; the guts to get beneath the surface of tough realities; and the heart to take heat and grief."

> *BM: If board members are not comfortable raising a point, I do it. And, hopefully, that then leads to more than one person flagging a concern. And we can have some healthy debate around that. So, I think that's the role of a Chair: to make sure that the issues are brought up and discussed openly.*

Having Good Judgment

Which Chair does not claim to have a sound judgment? We know from psychology that we tend to overrate ourselves. But, independent of our self-assessment, sound judgment is essential for a Chair—several personality traits listed in this chapter support solid judgment. Being a values-based person provides an excellent framework for judgment calls. If you are further willing to reflect on your behavior and even values—as in my authenticity example—you add another essential quality. Having sound self-esteem—not focusing on your energy to protect yourself and thereby narrow your awareness—combined with being humble enough to listen to others and understand different perspectives increases your chances of solid judgment. By displaying those qualities, you can digest and rank different signals quickly. One other essential ingredient: in the end, someone has to decide. Don't try to please. Leadership is about making decisions—what to do and what not to do.

Summarizing and Framing

If we encourage debate, it may lead to lengthy discussions in the wrong area.

> BM: The Chair must also be able to produce the synthesis in the meeting; he must have the gift of summarizing the result of a discussion relatively off the cuff.

> BM: The danger is that it will become an overflowing discussion club. The Chair must have the skill to react, summarize, and come to a decision at the appropriate moment. There is a beautiful phrase, "everything has already been said, but not by everyone." That not yet of all must be stopped from the Chair.

To summarize precisely and show appreciation for the participants, especially those with an outsider contribution, is a differentiating quality of a Chair. It takes language skills, sufficient understanding of the content, consideration of feelings, moderating the discussion, and taking a confident content lead.

> BM: One of the underestimated challenges of a Chair is that you can assert the authority to step up and bring a debate to a meaningful conclusion if you have pretty infringed perspectives around the table.

Maybe less common is the knowledge that framing is also essential. My last boss told me to put more emphasis on framing; I am easily bored if someone dwells on framing and tend to be too brief in articulating the assumptions or beliefs about a situation. Framing happens automatically and is neither good nor bad. But we should be aware that our frame is not anybody else's.

Our personal history and social context shape our frame. Still, according to Edmondson (2012), "we tend to assume that our framing represents the truth" rather than representing just our image of reality. We should not assume that everybody has the same or even a similar understanding of the task. Being aware of our frame makes it easier to recognize when we prioritize specific points over others. As a manager or board member, it is crucial to learn which issues to give more or less weight to and be aware of that complex process. Only awareness allows us to frame well because we know that different frames are available, potentially leading to different decisions. Framing needs attention that there is more than one frame, and we should reflect upon our own (Schön 2017).

Especially in board meetings, where the enormous amount of information is often not accompanied by a clear statement of expectation, framing is essential. Whether the Chair or the CEO does the framing is of no particular importance, but they are well advised to discuss in advance who does what: respect for all participants deserves preparing the framing as much as anything else.

Real Example

I end the chapter with a real-life example of one of my interviewees who showed many of the strengths I covered in this chapter: being reflective, being humble, managing relationships by showing empathy, not avoiding a conflict, and sticking to your values.

> *BM: I was the Chair in a male-dominated area, and I had a CEO who I felt was always opposing me. I had a growing feeling that he just didn't appreciate me leading the board because I was female. If I said "A," he said "B." I wondered why he was acting like this. Is something going on which triggers that behavior? Is he in a divorce? Is it his basic attitude? Is he biased? Am I overly sensitive? Do I trigger his behavior?*
>
> *Against my natural inclination, I did not just address the issue. It seemed awkward, and I didn't want to be put in the corner of a*

woman who reduces a problem with a man to a gender issue. I was reflecting, talking to my husband, and validating my assumptions. Unfortunately, my initial feelings and thoughts were confirmed, and I was ready to ask for help: Who's the best guy I have on my board to talk to this guy? Then, I said to this colleague: I think he has a problem with female leadership. Can you engage in a conversation with him to better understand where he's coming from and whether I am right? I didn't want to jump to conclusions myself without having tested the water first.

It turned out that he had an issue with working mums. Consequently, I organized a 1:1 meeting in which I addressed the issue directly in a respectful manner. I made it indubitably clear that each of us has a role to play, "this is my role, that's your role," and that professional behavior requires us together to find a reasonable way to deal with his bias in a win–win manner.

I was very conscious not to create losers. To have empathy and situational awareness in these kinds of situations is of utmost importance. An attitude of winning, anger, and emotion could have jeopardized the relationship and hence a possible way forward.

PART II
Board Interactions

CHAPTER 4

Scope and Structure

The future belongs to those who believe in the beauty of their dreams.
—Eleanor Roosevelt

Your visions will become clear only when you look into your heart; who looks outside, dreams; who looks inside awakes.
—Carl Gustav Jung

Scope

I will start with some preliminary remarks about the legal, cultural, and factual framework for the interactions at the top.

My experience stems primarily from Switzerland and boards in Germany, France, the United Kingdom, and Belgium.

Writing about boards, one can't help dropping a few lines about *the two-tier versus the one-tier structure*. The United States exemplifies the one-tier board, where the board of directors comprises both executive and nonexecutive members and therefore combines supervision and management responsibilities in one body. The most famous two-tier example is Germany, where the supervisory board and management board are organizationally separated. From a *legal perspective*, Switzerland has a one-tier structure; in reality, there is a hybrid structure that allows great flexibility. Executive directors are seldom also members of the board of directors. Switzerland has a high proportion of independent directors: according to Shekshnia and Zagieva (2019), SMI companies, which make up the largest companies in Switzerland, had 84 percent. It is common that the CEO, and often the executive board members, participate in board meetings on many agenda points.

In Europe, the United Kingdom's influence on European legislation and capital market regulation have softened the two-tier structure's former differences from the one-tier structure (Kalss 2020).

Although educated as a lawyer, I would not overestimate the influence of a two-tier versus a one-tier structure for group dynamics at the top.

Germany is the outlier, having a two-tier structure and compulsory employee participation on the board of directors, half-half, or two-thirds to one-third, depending on the size of the company. The frequency and intensity of interactions between the Chair and executive board in Germany are typically much lower than in most other countries where I conducted interviews.

What about *cultural differences* across nations? I was surprised that even my interviews in Latin America, which is, in the terminology of Erin Meyer (2014) and my own experience from Brazil, a highly relationship-driven and not task-oriented region, confirmed reluctance to be personal and open in senior business relationships.

Although my number of interviews is too small for definitive conclusions, I observed that women more than men, younger people more than older, and incumbents with less prestigious positions more than the top positions showed more willingness to enter the territory of working on professional relationships.

Having conducted interviews in around 20 countries, there was a pretty consistent picture. As much as I am fascinated by cultural differences, international boards seem to act in quite similar ways.

Confirming my experiences, in their research of Chairs' board practices across Europe, Shekshnia and Zagieva (2019) concluded that company characteristics (type of ownership, size, presence of executive and nonexecutive directors, financial health or life cycle) "have a stronger differentiating impact on what Chairs do than national or cultural differences."

What about the structural role of the Chair? Has the Chair an executive position or not? Is there an independent lead director? Or does one person combine the roles of the Chair and the CEO, as in many companies in the United States? That dynamic changes the overall picture.

However, the growing trend in the United States to employ a separate Chair and CEO brings them more in line with their European counterparts. The percentage of Stoxx Europe 600 companies with the roles combined was below 10 percent in 2018. In 2005, the United States had more than two-thirds combined Chair/CEO roles; by 2018, it was below 50 percent (Sun 2019).

I experienced extensive periods with a combined Chair/CEO role and found it worked well. Nevertheless, I do favor separation. I will not dwell on the different possibilities with, for example, an independent lead director. An overview of international roles is provided by Kakabadse and Kakabadse (2008). This book is written from the perspective of separate roles for Chair and CEO. I believe that globalization and the international setup of boards are leveling differences. We are all human beings, and our common denominator may be greater than we assume, especially if we focus on relational issues between the players at the top.

Structure

Figure 4.1 shows the relational web between the key players. Since the Chair and the CEO have unique roles within their respective teams, each has a separate box.

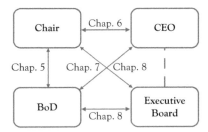

Figure 4.1 Board interactions

This book covers all interactions except that between the CEO and the executive board, which is the most intense and probably the most important for the company's well-being but also the most straightforward. Most leadership literature can be applied to the executive board, and most behavioral issues covered here can also be applied to the CEO and her team. The interactions between the board of directors, and the CEO and the executive board will be combined in one chapter.

CHAPTER 5

Interactions Between the Chair and the Board

You have two ears and one mouth; use them in proportion.
—Old proverb

If there is no tension, then you're not serious about what you're doing.
—Wynton Marsalis

Introduction

As in previous chapters, I assume a contemporary Chair who wants a strong board team and is willing to form one, even if it makes meetings more challenging.

Demanding that board members engage in constructive conflict, avoid destructive conflict, and work together sounds good in theory—but how can a Chair form a functioning, strong board team? Board members tend, as colleagues do, to suppress debates and, as a result, conflict aversion sets in. Knowing that boards are full of powerful, successful, and opinionated people, this attitude may be unexpected but, understanding the needs of teams and team members (see Chapter 2), it is not entirely surprising.

We generally overestimate board members' knowledge and awareness of their roles and underestimate their psychological needs.

BM: When I joined the board, I did not know what to expect or how to behave; I felt pretty insecure.

BM: Members are strong individuals, highly remunerated, with a track record. Entering a board, all those alpha animals have rough edges and a certain claim to leadership. Then you get into a board that is supposed to function as a collective, so how do I manage to tame a gang of Arabian stallions and make them all run in the same direction? Without, so to speak, losing the value, the power that sits there.

Entire Board (To Do's)

I have listed in Figure 5.1 what a Chair should do to form a strong team. Many topics are heavily linked and overlap.

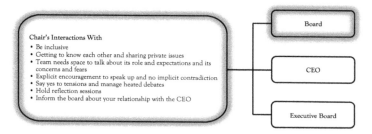

Figure 5.1 *Chair's interaction with the entire board*

Be Inclusive

Several board members stated that "feeling included" is essential; however, the motivation to be inclusive can have very different origins.

> BM: *Being included and being inclusive are both very important for me. Additionally, I remember how I felt when I joined the first board; I was very insecure and did not know what I should expect and what was expected from me. Then I recently got my first Chair position; I made sure that all felt welcome and belonging to that board team.*

For some being *inclusive* is a core value; it is vital to feeling included and include others. However, what we provide and what we want to receive do not always match. You can be a control freak but hate to be controlled yourself; you want to be included but including others does not come naturally.

The FIRO-B (Fundamental Interpersonal Relationship Orientations-Behavior) test measures interpersonal needs concerning inclusion, control, and affection. The "expressed" dimension shows to which extent you initiate that behavior, and the "wanted" dimension shows to which extent you want that behavior in others. My experience with the FIRO-B is that we generally want more inclusion and affection than expressing ourselves (with the control dimension being the opposite). Dunne (2019) talks about "asymmetric sensitivity," meaning that we demand greater sensitivity from others than we are prepared to give. This behavior is consistent with what we have seen in Chapter 2: the feeling of attachment and belonging to a group is a key human need we do wisely not to underestimate, as unlikely it may be that those needs are publicly acknowledged in a board setting. It is undoubtedly correct to assume that the feeling of "being included" is essential for board members.

> BM: *The board is honestly comparable to a kindergarten—they all need a lot of attention, appreciation, and inclusion. You have to listen carefully to their concerns if you don't want to run the risk of a silent board.*

> BM: *If you end up with a decision that you have been sort of steamrolling through and you've got a couple of people on the board who are pretty unhappy with this, then you may win the battle, but there is going to be a further problem down the line.*

While the first quote in this subchapter expressed the personal significance of the value of inclusion, the quotes above show more a rational motivation to act inclusively. A rationale, however different reason, to act inclusively is also expressed by the following two quotes:

> BM: *The big difference is that you, as a board member, are not authorized to give instructions to your board members; you are not the superior. You are, of course, the primus inter pares. But these people are all elected by shareholders, so I have to—and this is very exciting—deal with them differently to achieve a goal than when I am CEO and can tell my people I want it that way. And that's something different; I have to involve and reach a consensus to come to a decision. So, you need social competence and style to do it. You have to be inclusive.*

BM: As a former CEO and now a Chair, I learned that a board is much more a horizontal experience than a management team. You have to make an effort to include them all.

A more generic area where we should not underestimate the need to feel included is to bring *innovation and change* to a company. A famous old saying goes: "You have to go slow to go fast." As one executive chair said, talking about his lessons learned:

BM: The most significant challenge the board had to overcome was the "organizational tissue rejection," which is the phenomenon where existing staff create a toxic environment such that the new talents do not succeed and leave. Insurance colleagues used industry-specific acronyms; they did not welcome new digital colleagues and did not create a collaborative environment to integrate new ideas with the old ones. I learned that we—as change agents—didn't include our insurance colleagues enough to bring them on the journey. We made the classic mistake of creating this perception that anyone from the digital native environment was superior. In trying to promote digital, we unintentionally created this very unhealthy culture where someone from Amazon was deemed an expert in defining the future model. The insurance subject matter expert was sort of swept aside. That was a toxic culture, and it took us a little while to figure that out. We needed the insurance guys and the board to get engaged and make everyone feel important, spending time and effort to make sure the collaboration happened.

Having been responsible for leading strategy and digital transformation over the last few years, this quote resonates strongly. In an article about corporate startups (Sieber 2019b), I wrote that those who push innovative ideas within a group "are well-advised to act as humble advocates for their purpose" and share the spotlight with the core business. This may not always be easy, but it promises acceptance.

Feeling included is crucial, not only for the core business but also for the board. As a manager, you are usually dedicated to something and get to know it intimately, whereas for the board members, it is new, and they need time to digest further information. This may be a different form of inclusion, but it goes back to the same fundamental human need.

BM: As a Chair, you have to be completely open with boards—especially on strategic issues; you have to take a back seat to some extent so as not to come to the table already with fait accompli.

BM: The board is the highest authority, and it is a collegial body; this means that opinions should also arise and grow in the board; as Chair, I was proud when the board added content; then, it is also easier for the board to take ownership.

Inclusion also asks to put your ego aside: this is especially true for management and sometimes the Chair. Allowing the board to be co-owner and being open to their input is inclusive behavior.

I can share a personal example of being inclusive with the board.

Personal Example

I was newly elected as Chair of the supervisory board of two German insurance companies—life and nonlife—where I had previously been a board member and where employee representatives are also on the supervisory board. We had a complicated past with employee representatives and the Works Council in particular. Life and nonlife had different employee representatives on the supervisory boards; otherwise, they were composed of the same people. We had completely separate supervisory board meetings, even though the vast majority of topics were the same, so the management had to present twice: not an appealing situation either from efficiency or from an emotional perspective.

When I took over as Chair, I talked with the CEO and told him that I would like to involve the employee representatives more closely. We were often unable to implement the desired measures or could do so only after a long delay. I wanted to give the employee representatives a voice and provide more opportunities to express how they experienced the company. I also wanted to have a private session without the executive board to exchange ideas on the supervisory board.

While the CEO shared the desire to merge the meetings, he opined that this issue had no chance of success. He would not entertain the idea of the private session. I replied that the attempt alone was worth something, even if the employee representative rejected the proposal. The employee representatives agreed that we should merge the majority of the meetings. We also introduced a preboard meeting that took place without the executive board.

We saved a lot of time, but more importantly, we experienced a different atmosphere in those meetings: less formal, more open dialog.

This example shows that things can change if you, as Chair, are willing to listen to your board members. We all want to be included and feel appreciated. With employees' representatives as board members, the German participation board is unique, but there is a universal need to feel included.

I have not touched upon gender or the broader questions about diversity. But it seems evident that inclusion will only become more critical with a desired wider diversity on boards and new legislation, as in California, to include board members from underrepresented communities. Being inclusive makes a difference; it makes your members feel welcome and safe.

In the business context, inclusion sometimes still has a negative connotation; it is sometimes considered the opposite of efficiency. Inclusion does not mean that everybody participates every time. Such an attitude often has at its root a lack of trust. I once said in an executive board meeting when we discussed being inclusive versus being efficient: the best way to show inclusion is to think about my needs and concerns in a project meeting when I am not present.

Getting to Know Each Other and Sharing Private Issues

Feeling included is particularly relevant for new board members and helps with their integration.

BM: I did receive some onboarding, but it was more about facts and figures of the company; but I did not know much about my role as a board member—how to be an effective board member. I signed up for a couple of training which were helpful. But the decisive factor for a successful onboarding was that I embraced my insecurity, and I asked their advice a lot. I asked the Chair and other board members if my comments were valuable. I wanted them to know that I wanted to learn to be an effective board member.

Getting feedback is extremely difficult during regular meetings, which have a schedule with a fixed time frame. Beatty (2012) calls the boardroom an "unnatural and inhibiting environment."

The meeting and travel restriction due to COVID-19 makes it harder to get to know ourselves. One interviewee introduced a monthly "happy hour" where the team members meet.

BM: It is not compulsory to participate. We talk about anything but business; it helps us connect, get to know ourselves better, and feel safer— as a consequence, we are more open to address critical issues later.

Knowing other board members on a personal level was seen as an advantage. Business trips where you have time for one-on-one talks with somebody to get to know the person are beneficial, as are informal dinners before the board meeting.

BM: I attach great importance to personal contact. We always meet in the evening before. Anyone who has time comes. There is no compulsion. This gives you a personal basis, family knowledge, and the safe feeling that you belong to that body. We deliberately also do purely social events—even with partners. This is a good thing and does not cost a lot of money. It makes it easier to participate, to have a say later in the board meeting. Everyone has mutual trust.

Getting to know each other builds trust, especially vital in a crisis or a potential crisis.

BM: The barrier to call or to address a critical issue is lowered.

BM: You also know, then, critical prior events in a board member's life, which can help a lot to understand why he is acting as he is.

BM: The better you know somebody, the easier it is to read nonverbal clues, which are also important.

BM: If you share private issues, it is like paying into a human toler-ance account. If nothing is in there, you can't withdraw anything in a crisis.

As seen in Chapter 2, the Google experiment and my INSEAD thesis confirmed that sharing private issues increases team members' psycholog-ical safety and therefore speaking up.

My interviewees supported getting to know other board members but raised concerns if the Chair's buddies are selected because those old loy-alties may promote silence and hinder open dialogue (see the subsection about the Nomination Committee in this chapter).

Questions regarding sharing private issues triggered generally positive reactions, though some were ambivalent, expressing concerns about los-ing appropriate professional distance.

BM: Boards should not be the best friends, but you should like each other, like coming together and going for a beer after a meeting. It is nec-essary to find the right balance and maintain an appropriate relation-ship and degree of contact: board members should not be "best mates."

This concern is valid and can be summarized as "groupthink," where team members strive for an early consensus without testing different ideas. Groupthink can lead to a more silent board because members don't want to disturb the overall harmony (Janis 1982; Edmondson 2012). It is like the hedgehog parable: How much closeness is too close? It is about finding the right balance. I will come back in more detail to that point of intimacy and boundaries writing about the Chair–CEO relationship in Chapter 6.

Let me close this section with an excellent example from an interview:

BM: On one occasion in a multinational company, a friend of mine received an e-mail request for information from a stranger, a colleague in another country. To carry out the demand would have created a lot of work but would not have produced any valuable information. My friend was adamant that the writer was an idiot and was trying to screw up his life! I knew the e-mail writer but asked my friend: "How many real idiots does the company employ?"

Answer: "Very few."

BM: "If this person does not know you, why would he be trying to screw up your life?"

Answer: "Good point!"

BM: "We then phoned the writer of the e-mail, and everything was quickly resolved."

The BM continued: "Suppose we take our call today. We didn't know each other, but after the interview, we will have a certain level of trust, making our future interactions more comfortable. So, I want to say that without much time invested, we can move from suspicion as a starting point to somewhat trustful; it makes it more likely that we will react positively to each other. Sure, to get more intimacy, it needs time, but just to get to know each other a little makes a big difference in how we collaborate."

Boards must make room for their members to get to know each other and feel more comfortable by organizing informal events like company visits, retreats, or social gatherings. The so-called "noncontent time" may be more effective (and significant) than our education has led us to believe.

A Team Needs Time and Space to Talk About Its Role and Expectations and Its Concerns and Fears

This heading is broad and in many ways a precursor for others. Because it is crucial but often neglected, I decided to include it as a heading nonetheless.

Talk about roles and expectations or fears and concerns doesn't receive enough attention at the management level and even less on the board. Management is busy getting their job done; at the board level, a lack of experience with such conversations may combine with the fear of Pandora's box that might be opened. So, these topics are often avoided, especially those about fears and concerns.

A positive outlier was the following quote:

BM: And frankly, we'd like to spend more time on that and flesh out the issues earlier rather than later. One of the worst things is when a board doesn't talk about what's bothering them. I think that's very unhealthy. My challenge as a Chair is to try hard to ensure that everybody raises their concerns early and openly.

As we have seen in the introduction and Chapter 2, it's hard for board members to find their place. Struggling to do so can result in dysfunctional behavior. You can be too silent (shy, unsure if you add value, not knowing if your contribution is welcome) or too active. In one of the interviews, a Chair complained about one board member who was always intensely focused on governance and compliance issues.

> BM: *"It is frustrating for all of us, including him. He regularly presses compliance points but gets turned down. But it does bother me and keeps me awake at night sometimes—thinking about whether we have taken the right decision and whether I treated him correctly."*
>
> Me: *"Have you talked to this board member? How does he experience the board meetings?"*
>
> BM: *"Sometimes, we talk, and it feels good for both of us, but in most cases, we are too tired after the board meeting, and then weeks after weeks pass, and we both let it slip."*
>
> Me: *"What reasons could the board member have to stress the compliance points?"*
>
> BM: *"Maybe, he wants to add value and have an impact; be recognized for his field of expertise; maybe I don't provide enough appreciation, but honestly, we have never touched the topic of what could be behind his attitude."*
>
> Me: *"What else could be a reason for his behavior?"*
>
> BM: *"Oh…Maybe he had a bad experience in the past with a compliance issue."*

Maybe the board member just feels that compliance issues don't get enough attention, or had a negative experience with one, or strives for appreciation, feeling the urge to contribute. Whatever the reasons are to press those issues, the way it is done consumes time and frustrates all involved, but the problem still has not been addressed. I would suggest talking to that board member about it in a broader context, not just about a specific content issue.

The exchange shows that you may have anxieties and be unable to talk about them. Your behavior helps neither the company nor yourself. Therefore, you need to talk about roles and expectations and, hopefully, you as a team can also address insecurities, fears, and concerns.

> *BM: I learned that it doesn't matter how senior or experienced an individual is; every human being still has insecurities. And when you're invited on to a board, there's this human psychology that you need to have all the right answers. When you're doing something brand new, like starting a new digital enterprise, no one has the answer. So, the right way is to embrace the fact as an individual and as a team that you don't have all the answers. Only then can you create an environment where people are courageous enough to try new things and learn.*

Addressing issues requires constant deliberation, not automated responses. Some points regarding roles and expectations are best covered in the selection and onboarding processes. As a rule, I recommend that each Chair meet each board member individually once or twice a year. This can serve many purposes (getting to know each other better, showing appreciation, room for exchange—see subsection between the meetings in this chapter). You should also provide the team with space to talk about roles and expectations, committee work, and the kind of collaboration and dialogue you want to have as a team.

As a Chair, you should *articulate your expectations* and ask about their expectations and concerns.

One newly elected Chair started his first board meeting with the following questions:

1. What are my expectations toward the performance of that board?
2. What are my concerns or fears when I am joining the board?
3. How can I potentially support the board dynamics?

4. How can I potentially hinder the board dynamics?

The Chair had not asked the board in advance to conduct such an exercise.

> BM: *It was an unusual exercise for that board, and not all board members liked the session, but it created a bond between the board members which will help us in the future.*

I like this openness and courage. It should not be a one-time event. An excellent place to collect issues is the reflection sessions at the end of the board meeting (see the section about "hold reflection sessions" in this chapter).

As your expectations may run against some deep-rooted beliefs and concerns (see Chapter 2 and the following subsection, "the need for repetitive and explicit encouragement"), you have to be clear and consistent in your communication. You should ask your board members what they need from you or other board members to show the desired behavior. Listen well, even for what is unsaid. Depending on the topic and the team's maturity, some critical issues may not come up, but be clear that you have an open ear.

As a Chair, your role is critical. However, board members can also create an open atmosphere by asking other board members about their views. Human beings like to be asked; several board members said that it is astonishing that such behavior is rarely practiced (*BM:* "*to throw a ball into somebody's court*") and needs to be supported by the Chair as well:

> BM: *If the Chair is not a role model who encourages openness, the initiatives of other colleagues will sooner or later come to a halt.*

Board members should be encouraged to *participate and speak up, address questions to other members,* and try to *build on each other's contributions.* Listening and mirroring show that somebody has been heard, a different kind of engagement that improves the thinking process of the speaker. It is the opposite of our everyday behavior, as Stephen Richard's Covey quote says pointedly: "Most people do not listen with the intent to understand; we listen with the intent to reply."

In my recent years as executive manager, we have started to apply the concept of the *integrated decision-making process*. The idea goes back to Robertson (2016) and follows a strict procedure where, after the initial presentation, each team member can ask only clarification questions (not give opinions or first positions). A reaction round follows, where everybody talks in a predetermined order. The presenter can then make adjustments and, in the end, asks if anybody has a veto. In particular, the exact order of speaking improves listening quality, as everybody is heard, and knowing when it's your turn enhances listening quality (Kline 1999). A structured process, separating thinking from deciding, has several advantages (listening, equal participation) but can take longer, and you still need time to discuss the key points.

But why not experiment once? According to Edmondson (2012), experimentation is a vital aspect of teaming because of the inherent uncertainty in the interdependent action. It signals to the team that you allow, and are open to, uncertainty; as a board team, you have somewhat limited options with which to experiment.

If you follow the first points in that chapter—*be inclusive, talk about your roles, and provide room to get to know each other*—you have a great chance to create trust, psychological safety, and an engaged board.

> *BM: We discussed how we function as a team and become a high-performance team and not "a bunch of individuals" sitting around the table.*

Explicit Encouragement to Speak Up and No Implicit Contradiction

While talking about roles, expectations, fears, and concerns lays out the basis for a functioning board and open dialogue, the *explicit encouragement to speak up* earns its own section because of its importance. One of the key findings of my INSEAD thesis (Sieber 2019a) was that psychological safety is necessary, but not sufficient, to create a behavior of speaking up. Board members can feel safe but do not speak up; they need to be explicitly and repetitively encouraged to show speaking-up behavior (see Chapter 2, step 4/6).

The interviewees underlined the view that board members need repeated, explicit encouragement to speak up, confirming the study's quantitative results, and stressed the Chair's role in creating a culture where speaking up is desired.

BM: The board needs encouraging and motivational leadership to enable "a speaking-up" culture.

BM: I often state my view at the end.

BM: A Chair should not talk much but should motivate others to get involved.

BM: I ask quiet board members for their opinion; board members learn fast, and they realize that I expect that they are prepared and participate actively.

BM: Yes, I try to give people the feeling that it is desirable to formulate their opinion, to make a proactive contribution.

BM: Most valuable were boards where the Chair invited the individual members to give their opinions before directing the decision-making process with his statement. The idea develops with the collection of different views. I think such invitations to active participation are a crucial thing.

BM: Especially the Chair has to act as a role model in appreciating contradictory opinions; my board has regularly experienced me acting like this, and my attitude has had some catching up effect on others.

BM: She has excellent things to say, and once she gets going, she's very persistent and good, but she does need some encouragement to speak sometimes, and I make sure that I ask her.

The need for explicit encouragement could be that *implicit beliefs discourage speaking up* (see Chapter 2, step 4/6). Although Chairs have little choice about whether board members bring these implicit beliefs into their boardroom, they should explicitly communicate that speaking-up behavior is desired. Sometimes board members perceive that the Chair does not want a debate in the board room, and sometimes we know that this is not just a perception but reality.

> *BM: I was on the board of a technology company. The Chair was an engineer who strictly followed his scheduled time; whenever we had a good discussion, he felt an urgency to move to the next subject. Sometimes—in retrospect probably too often—I said: "Sorry, this is essential now; we shouldn't stop right here." Maybe I was naïve, perhaps I did it in the wrong way, or the Chair simply thought that I wasn't pragmatic, but my speaking up resulted in my mandate not being renewed.*

Commonly, Chairs were unsure how explicit they made the invitation to have a debate. Make it *very explicit* and repeat it:

> *BM: I think I made it clear that I like to have debates. [Hesitating] I mean, I made it clear to people individually—I am not sure if I specifically addressed it in the full board.*

Explicit language is essential, but board members must perceive that the encouragement is genuine and body language matches. Board members, as human beings, are well trained to perceive nonverbal clues. What is unsaid can enact a spiral of the "unsaid known" (Engbers 2020). Several board members made statements that everyone, especially the Chair, needs to control their nonverbal signals. Reading nonverbal cues is of enormous importance, but sending out the wrong ones *"can be deadly" (BM).* It is sometimes tempting to make signals to another board member, but the harm can be substantial. In particular, *"the Chair should not roll his eyes or glare discouragingly" (BM).* Nonverbal cues or nonblaming language are crucial in engendering voice behavior (Geertshuis 2015; Garvin and Roberto 2001).

As a board member, you are likely attached to your mandate for economic or social reasons, so you don't stand up to the Chair or CEO or you don't want to feel embarrassed and expose yourself, making for a rather quiet board member. Board members, particularly the Chair, have to reduce or eliminate these hurdles as far as possible to encourage a culture of debate. Even if it seems self-evident that negative explicit incentives should be avoided, it is not always the rule, as these two quotes demonstrate:

> *BM: The subject of censorship by the Chair is a severe issue. I was once on a board of directors that a university professor chaired. He gave a grade every time a board member made a statement; he couldn't help it. It was his attitude, but you can imagine what the result was.*

> *BM: One little remark can be deadly: the Chair says, "that could have been read," or the CEO who provides us with 1000 pages and then says, "yes, on page 67, we wrote that." Such "little" remarks can destroy a lot.*

The Chair should not take for granted that board members will address critical issues; board members may not feel safe to do so and, even feeling safe, may not know if such a behavior is desirable. The Chair must explicitly encourage open debate, act as a role model in allowing different opinions, and foster a culture where no implicit harmful signals censor other board members.

Say Yes to Tensions and Manage Heated Debates

Managing debate on the board is crucial, which I have already addressed as a necessary personality trait for the Chair (see Chapter 3). Here, I will focus more on the practical aspects.

While nobody disputes that you can have the wrong tension, *"merely a distraction and leads to having frustrated board members" (BM)*, many boards seem to lack the understanding that tensions are necessary. It is the task of the Chair to be very explicit that conflicts are needed to perform well.

> *BM: In my board experience, a managed conflict is better than a sleeping battle and I make sure that my board knows my attitude.*

This quote does not correspond to the overall behavior in boardrooms; many board members may be happy if conflicts are cleared before specific topics reach the boardroom. My interviews showed a considerable variety of opinions on whether a Chair should align with the CEO before the board meeting or whether the Chair should contribute independently like any other board member.

> BM: We try to avoid any significant disagreement during a board session, so I am aligned with the CEO when the proposals come to the board.

> BM: Normally, I am aligned with the CEO; if I have a different opinion and we could not find a common view, she knows that I will express my opinion, so she will not be surprised.

> BM: The biggest problem for Chairs and CEOs is that the two of them have a predefined solution when the topic enters the board room.

> BM: Chairs should have their opinions and should have good judgment. So, entering a board meeting, you may have the "perfect" solution in your head, but it is crucial for the board as a team that you are willing to learn and adapt your answer if the right arguments are put in front of you.

It seems evident that it is harder to engender a serious debate if the Chair and executive board are tightly aligned beforehand. The more independent from your executive team you act as a Chair, the more open discussions you will have in the boardroom. As a general rule, the more strategic a topic, the more dialogue you should encourage. The stronger you want your board to be involved, the less you should seek agreement in advance. It also makes a big difference if you have time to get the board's input and decide later on or if you need to settle the issue in the upcoming session.

Independent of how strongly you as a Chair are aligned with the CEO, it is crucial to stay open to new arguments and avoid "known" surprises for the management.

> BM: Conflicts are excellent and healthy per se. Sometimes, the reality is different. Often the presentations have already been combed through 10 times; everything is slick and smooth, then you don't discuss it.

If presentations are too sanitized, it is even more challenging for the board to grasp the subject. The more strategic and vital a topic, the more crucial it is to lay out the arguments. Management should be encouraged to state where they debated and be transparent with pros and cons. But laying out the arguments for all minor decisions may invite good discussions about the wrong issues.

If you follow the recommendation in the previous chapter, you already have encouraged speaking up. You have to facilitate difficult conversations if you are serious about it; otherwise, it won't lead to anything different. If you say "yes" to difficult conversations, you must acknowledge emotional reactions.

> *BM: I believe that sins triggered by openness and passion—by speaking up—are less harmful than sins out of cowardice, gutlessness, or ill will.*

> *BM: Also, board members have to really care about the purpose, and if you deeply care about the meaning of the company, then you have emotions. I would rather see board members displaying more emotions openly and honestly.*

If you feel emotionally close to your organization (have passion and engagement), you are more likely to speak up. But since it is only a part-time job, we should not take board member engagement for granted.

> *BM: How do I ensure that my board thinks day and night about what is best for the company?*

Showing emotion is a sign of engagement and passion and also provides data. Emotions shape the decision-making process on boards as much as in any other area in our life, so we should try to make them explicit instead of leaving them as unspoken biases (Davey, in Goleman et al. 2017). But if you show emotion, your fellow board members must perceive it as engagement in the company's success and not in winning, especially in a culture where heated debate is not the rule. If your peers do not get that feeling or, worse, if they don't see the relevance, they might think you are riding a hobbyhorse (Heifetz, Grashow, and Linsky 2009).

BM: We need a passion for the company; we need to be fundamentally interested in somebody else, and the company is somebody else—it is not about me; if passion wins over ego, then we develop a good debate and struggle for the best solution. We need a passion for the good cause of the company and not for egos to win.

If a team explicitly acknowledges emotions and conflicts, it already allows us to perceive a heated debate with different lenses. Not every battle is terrible; maybe two board members are just searching for the best, not the easiest, solution. Consciously saying "yes" to tension helps board members focus on what is happening instead of taking an attitude where the brain is preoccupied with negative feelings, wishing for harmony as soon as possible. Often, if somebody gets emotional, they feel misunderstood, so we should make an effort to listen and, if appropriate, ask clarifying questions.

Communication and observation skills are critical tools in conflicts. As a Chair, keep the team focused on the shared goal by articulating and repeating it from time to time. If you, or your team members, can help manage conflicts (see Chapter 2) and combine thoughtful statements and questions that help understand the factual bases of disagreement and determine the rationale behind it, your chances of having productive conflicts will increase (Edmondson 2012).

Every board member can work on how and when issues are addressed: tone and timing come into play. According to neuro-linguistic programming specialists, the words themselves, in any communication, provide roughly only a third of the meaning. This is one effect that we are missing right now with video calls. This leads to Jen Hogan's statement in her blog (www.sakurapro/blog.com): "It wasn't what you said, it was the way you said it," *which* can make a big difference in how your statement is perceived.

BM: I have learned to wrap my points more in a question form which seems to trigger fewer adverse reactions.

Open questions empower the person who is to answer. They leave choice and deliver trust because you give up some control of the situation.

But not everything should be formulated as a question. If you have a clear opinion, then state it, but keep in mind that the management should run the business. Don't hide behind others; formulate it as an "I." Not being a fact makes it less final and absolute; it can be discussed instead of decreed. We all are prone to naïve realism (see Chapter 2), believing that our view is more common than it is, which leads us to overoptimistically think that others share our view; when somebody disagrees, we tend to blame them (Edmondson 2012).

Don't confuse your opinion with fact, but also don't be so unclear that nobody understands your point. The opposite of a clear statement is to soften your comment so that the listener doesn't get the message or talk in such an abstract way that it doesn't help. This is not uncommon at the top because many leaders have a strong need to be liked and avoid doing anything that makes them less popular (Kets de Vries 2006). My experience is that the higher you are in the hierarchy, the more opaque language becomes, tending to be abstract or blurred, and not just because of excellent language skills. The board of directors is a paradise for blurred language regarding critical issues and not just by the board members themselves.

Personal Example

As a secretary of the board, I asked a manager after the audit committee meeting to share an observation. The audit committee members did not ask any questions after the manager spoke about a very technical issue which is not uncommon. I told the manager that what he said sounded great, but I did not get a grip on what he was saying and I was unsure if the board members understood him. So, I asked him what the board members will take away from his speech. He said that he didn't know. Then I asked him whether he believed he had spoken to help the board or with the intention of not being questioned.

It is typical behavior to talk so abstractly that it sounds impressive, but the listener is lost. It takes courage to ask a question: it may seem that everybody else understood or acts as if they have, or you don't want to indirectly attack the speaker by telling them that what they wanted to express was unclear. The Chair has an important role here:

> BM: I am very much for precise and direct language, even if it is sometimes not easy for one or the other, but it helps us. And if somebody is not clear, I explicitly ask for it.

Timing is also crucial:

> BM: Sometimes, it is better to sleep on something and not react immediately. Otherwise, relationships can turn sour.

Sometimes it is necessary to suspend your thoughts to allow the dialogue to develop. If you consider the speaker's context and personality further and focus on what is said, you will understand more and ask more powerful questions. Maybe you will miss the chance to say something, but with the benefit that others can speak (see reflection wheel in Chapter 2).

The "how" of addressing issues, the capacity to suspend your thoughts, and your statement's timing are all critical tools and techniques to make meetings more efficient and smooth. However, an engaged board will have more fierce and heated debates. We need to be prepared for this and aware that being engaged and passionate are essential ingredients for board members. But they also make it harder to suspend our thoughts to foster an open dialogue (Schein 1993). Therefore, we need to reflect on how we act as a team.

Hold Reflection Sessions

Reflection sessions usually take place after all agenda points are discussed. Private sessions, also called in-camera sessions, are sessions without management participation. Usually, they take place before the official board meeting starts to allow board members to address issues that they may be reluctant to air in the presence of the executive board.

In my INSEAD thesis (Sieber 2019a)—as opposed to my personal experience (see "Be Inclusive" in Chapter 5)—private sessions did not have any predictive effect on psychological safety or voice behavior. However, conducting reflection sessions had the highest positive impact on psychological safety and speaking-up behavior. Of course, one can always question such a result with the chicken-and-egg effect: Are boards that hold such sessions more reflective from the beginning? Are they more open in general?

The qualitative interviews showed a picture of older board members seeming to be less open for such sessions.

> *BM: I generally have trouble with reflection sessions; we all have the same shyness, so the results are dull.*

However, those who held formalized reflection sessions were very positive.

> *BM: In one board, we have a joint reflection after each board meeting but not in the sense of self-flagellation; it creates awareness that we should work as a team, it creates trust and bonding and therefore it certainly helps our speaking up and our overall performance.*

> *BM: Our reflection session after each board meeting also helps to let out accumulated heat, which is not released uselessly. Sometimes, I am astonished that board members are much more critical than I perceived during the decision-making process; it makes me uncomfortable to learn that only in the reflection session, but it demonstrates the importance of the reflection session to work on our culture—to be more composed in dealing with conflicting issues.*

Some boards conduct evaluations where the executive board provides feedback in a structured way to the board, and the board reflects upon it.

> *BM: I want to take them seriously, ask for their opinion explicitly and mobilize their thinking. We conduct extensive workshops to discuss elephants in the room, to talk about and reflect on ourselves. This led me to be less directive, which helps the team.*

I will revisit the importance of the executive board providing feedback to the entire board (Chapter 11).

The interviews painted a consistent picture: joint reflections are impossible or ineffective without the explicit endorsement and commitment of the Chair. On some boards, the Chair has one-to-one reflection meetings. While such talks serve many purposes, joint reflection sessions were considered more effective, especially when forming the board as a team.

Besides speaking up, collaboration, and experimentation, reflection is one of the four pillars of an effective team (Edmondson 2012). In line with my INSEAD thesis results (Sieber 2019a), I strongly encourage that each board holds reflection sessions; I dedicate Part III to reflection and board evaluation.

Inform the Board About Your Relationship With the CEO

Several Chairs expressed reasonable concerns about sharing information about their relationship with the CEO with the board and, as a consequence, did not share it at all.

> BM: I am not running to the board to complain about the CEO; that feels like stabbing a knife in the CEO's back. You can take the knife out, but a deep wound remains.

Others showed a cautious attitude to avoid appearing to throw the CEO under the bus.

> BM: I don't share everything and not immediately with the board; you have to think carefully about whether you want to bring something critical to the board; otherwise, I would quickly "break the CEO's baton."

Rather exceptional was the attitude of a Chair who stated:

> BM: I regularly share how it is going with the CEO; it does not take long. The board should know about how we are getting along.

Informing the board about your relationship with the CEO is the last section in this chapter, and you may wonder why I mention this point at all since the other topics in this chapter relate to the development of an effective team.

I would argue that informing the board about the most critical relationship in a company makes them feel included. In my corporate functions, I was surprisingly often asked about the Chair and the CEO's relationship, demonstrating a specific need of the board members to be informed on this subject—assuming the right motivation for the displayed curiosity.

I could also argue from a risk management perspective that the board should be aware of the Chair's relationship with the CEO, and questions around their relationship usually are part of the "state-of-the-art" board review (see Chapter 11).

However, the main reason for raising the point is that Chairs surprisingly often mentioned feeling isolated in dealing with behavioral issues with the CEO, in particular, if the results of the company are good.

Several Chairs told me that they got reactions from their board members such as:

- *It will be okay. Just be patient.*
- *It is not as bad as you may feel right now.*
- *We are doing well; you don't have to be the best buddy with the CEO.*
- *I know that she appreciates you.*

Whether those statements were true or, as some Chairs perceived, some board members were not interested in being drawn into such a muddy topic is a different question. Regardless, it is not ideal if Chairs feel unsupported in dealing with such vital issues.

However, I also heard several statements like:

BM: I have never felt in a position where I've been isolated on a board or could not talk about the CEO with another board member.

Having asked Chairs how they dealt with information about the CEO with the board, one thing was evident: those boards that were regularly informed about the Chair's relationship with the CEO were more open to, and better prepared to talk about, those issues if the relationship started to turn sour.

If a Chair only addresses the board when the relationship becomes difficult, the perception can be that the Chair is merely trying to elicit broader support to win the battle.

Well-informed board members who know about sensitive issues between the Chair and the CEO are also less likely to pour fuel on the fire in their interactions with the CEO.

To prevent being "lonely" in such an important matter, gain reflection partners, and reduce risks for the company, I recommend Chairs share the status of their relationship with the CEO regularly, even if the idea may go against their gut feeling. Particularly with a newly hired CEO, sharing information on the relationship is essential.

Since sharing also brings risks, what needs to be considered?

Sharing should not be accompanied by judging or hints of accusation. The Chair should not run to the board with every trivial issue or use it as a tactic to settle his nerves or create a positive reputational impact for himself. Especially, he should not use it as a tactic to undermine the CEO (see Chapter 6). The sharing should not be detailed and should be brief.

Sharing should not take the place of working on your relationship with the CEO. I strongly encourage you to work on your relationship with the CEO (see Chapter 6) and, as a default mechanism, try to address areas of concerns directly with her with an open mindset. Often, we worry more than necessary; don't problematize or wait too long. There may be no need to dramatize; there's always the possibility that there has been a misunderstanding.

If the issue does go deeper, take time to reflect; such a crucial relationship warrants reflection on your feelings and thoughts. If you are, for whatever reason, not sure how to proceed, talk to someone with an open and independent mind that you fully trust; explain the situation and ask how they would handle it?

Be aware of people who just reconfirm your opinion! The appropriate person is most likely a board member, somebody close to you in the organization, but it can also be someone outside the board that you trust. As a Chair, you should have, or seek out, such trusted people in your orbit to help you vent your thoughts and feelings, learn to see a new perspective, or test an appropriate reaction. Whatever you share, try to do it with an open, nonjudgmental mindset to gain new perspectives.

If you decide to share, take a gradual approach.

> *BM: I find it easier and more appropriate to share complex issues on an individual level first; you get new insights, and maybe the storm will pass, or you are preparing the ground on a one-to-one basis and then include more directors later.*

> *BM: I think talking to one individual can help you have a different perspective and realize the difficulty may not be as bad as you believe. This reduces the risk of doing unnecessary harm.*

> *BM: Unless it is bad behavior, I believe in treating people in general with sensitivity and generosity. If you have a particular issue, you talk with the CEO. If it is a persistent or deep-rooted issue, I like to speak first on a confidential basis with a nonexecutive board member to get his view and win different perspectives. Then—if necessary—you include more board members.*

I fully support being cautious but, for the reasons set out at the beginning of this section, I also favor an attitude of sharing regularly and early—not just when things get tricky.

How and when you share may differ, depending on whether the disagreement relates to a particular incident or an ongoing behavioral issue.

If you have a dispute regarding a specific *task or decision*, you may do more harm than good in taking an opposing stance with the CEO before you know the position of your board or at least some of your board members.

> *BM: We had a complicated situation related to the overall salary and incentive structure for the CEO. The way that I dealt with that was, in doing the negotiations, to make sure that I was not doing it by myself but also fully involved the head of the remuneration committee. Because it was difficult, we had many calls with the rest of the board to ensure we were all aligned on this.*

BM: I think it is wrong for a Chair to go charging in and potentially damage the relationship with the CEO quite severely and then for the board to have to deal with a significant problem. You could end up in a particular position that might not be the right outcome in the first place. If I see a problem coming over the horizon, I first reflect and then share it with some or all the nonexecutives on the board. Before I contemplated entering into some sort of big fight with the CEO, I would make sure that the rest of the board is aligned. Not doing so, you potentially destroy a lot and put the board into a situation that is ultimately inconsistent with what we might all agree. Where difficult and/or personal messages are involved, I would certainly make sure that two directors were involved to avoid clashes or miscommunication.

Getting alignment on the board is more crucial in areas where you, as Chair, have a clear responsibility, like remuneration. But aligning the directors in advance runs the risk of closing ranks too early, potentially robbing the CEO of the chance to argue her case; therefore, alignment with the board can also mean alignment on how to proceed.

Finally, let's assume that the relationship turns so sour that you have severe doubts that it is sustainable; it can become tempting to malign the CEO. Some experienced board members may have the capacity to smooth specific issues and act as a coach for the involved parties. But if the worst comes to the worst, the board is in an awkward situation and maybe inadequately prepared to judge who should stay and who should go.

In my interviews—mainly with Chairs—it was often the conclusion that it has to be the CEO who has to go. One Chair, however, pointed out rightfully that:

BM: It is one of the most challenging tasks for a board to decide whose replacement and succession are essential to the company's long-term success.

BM: If the relationship between CEO and Chair is fundamentally antagonistic, you have problems regardless of their relationship with the rest of the board. If the point is reached where that relationship has fundamentally broken down, then it is likely that somebody's got to go. But it should not be automatically the CEO.

One Chair even said:

BM: Nobody should be more important than the company. The CEO might be the most important person, but the company has to come first. Neither one is the boss of the other. The boss is the company. You need checks and balances. If they are fighting for supremacy—at least one has to go, maybe both.

Being aware that a lot depends on individual circumstances, bear in mind whatever and whenever you share, do it with an open mind, and with readiness to learn and gain new perspectives, not just to get confirmation of your own opinion. It makes a difference for all involved, including yourself, and shows a growth mindset.

Committees

Committees in General

Committees are today's best practice and, at least for certain companies, are even mandatory. Comparing the past with the present can be unfair since expectations and self-conception have changed toward a more active board. Nevertheless, it is fair to say that the creation of committees has led to better risk awareness and more engaged board members, with more specific tasks and more interactions with the executive board members and even the entire board.

Several interviewees reflected upon the idea of having a smaller board with more time spent on the mandate and potentially fewer committees. Many boards have between 8 and 12 members, making committee work indispensable. While audit/risk and compensation committees are the most common, most have nominations committees and some have strategy, investment, or people committees.

In Switzerland, some companies still have a Chair's committee, headed by the Chair of the board and some senior board members. This is usually the most important committee. Several interviewees stated that the Chair's committee should either be abandoned or restricted to extraordinary tasks or exist more for exceptional circumstances, such as a takeover, a situation with an activist shareholder, or a major M&A.

The Chair's committee should not serve as a preparatory committee for the board meeting or you will create dual-class citizenship within the board, a contradiction of the concept of having a strong team and open dialogue.

BM: The Chair's committee is outdated. Companies should get rid of it.

BM: We can discuss everything in the Chair's committee, which is excellent, but it indeed leads to a problematic situation for the rest; if the Chair's committee has reached an opinion, another board member needs a lot of courage and powerful arguments to state a different view. With some distance now, I judge the Chair's committee very critically.

BM: I only set up Chair's committees for very urgent temporary tasks to avoid the ordinary members of the board of directors' disengagement.

If you believe in maintaining a Chair's committee, then the Chair needs to be willing to present issues from it in such a way as to invite other members of the board the opportunity to ask questions and speak up, which can be challenging.

In general, committees provide a chance for interaction between board members and the executive board (see Chapter 8). How well board members can fulfill their role says much about the Chair's willingness to have a functioning board. A committee's margin to maneuver demonstrates whether the Chair sees their role as mainly for optics.

Committees also risk disengagement, especially if the briefing of work indicates that the decisions have been made already and that further discussion is discouraged.

BM: If I feel that the committees' decisions are predetermined, then I become miserable and speak up.

Most noncommittee board members tend to become silent about issues covered in a committee.

BM: The truth is that the issues that go to the committees lose the intrinsic value of the members who are not on the committees. The commitment to the problems loses because one (un)consciously knows the committee takes care of it. As a noncommittee member, you ask what I shall do here; it is all prediscussed?

By challenging another committee, you run the risk of being challenged in response and may be less likely to question to avoid interference in your area of responsibility. Such behavior is typical in executive teams.

Several board members claimed that they could not remember any conclusion made by a committee being overturned. If you work with committees, the inclusion of noncommittee members is crucial. Having roles fixed for an extended period does not call for a collaboration mindset; a few interviewees stated that they regularly rotate committee members.

What I have written about the board's roles and expectations is equally valid for committees. Each committee should discuss its task, the interaction between the Chair and the committee's head, and how the content should be briefed to the board. Each committee should also ask the board for their expectations and feedback. The appropriate way to handle briefing and interacting with the entire board and the Chair can be very different between companies and committees within the same company; one size does not fit all.

Several interviewees stated that heads of committees' briefing quality are variable. While they see room for improvement, they observe significant hesitation to address the subject. Many boards have not learned to talk about themselves. It is so much easier to talk about areas where others could improve, especially for the board, which has few tasks of its own. Being a role model for a learning attitude, the board should seriously talk about its areas for improvement. Reflection sessions or board reviews can be a helpful tool, provided the focus is on improving the collaboration, not grading performance (see Chapter 11).

The more strategic a topic is, the more time for open discussion with the board is justified. But that's not a rule since those topics are also more challenging for the board and management and they may be reluctant to enter into a debate with an unpredictable outcome. The more concrete the issue, the easier it is to have an opinion and dwell on it.

Naturally, committees can lead to irritation, especially if the committee head violates the Chair's authority's perceived, often unspoken, boundaries. Committees often have no power to make decisions, but, in some areas, the board can delegate formal authority to committees (especially for the compensation committee or the investment committee).

BM: If committees have delegated decision power, they should be transparent about the pros and cons and share if they were insecure or controversially discussed.

But even within delegated power, acting autonomously can be tricky. All participants need to be vigilant about the needs of others. For example, if the compensation committee wants to alter the CEO's bonus proposal and formally has the decision power to do so, I would advise the head of the committee to confirm with the Chair (who usually should not sit on the compensation committee).

You can also send significant signals to executive board members outside of formally holding power, something to be handled with sensitivity. I recommend that each committee head has open talks with the Chair about what is essential for both roles. Very similar to the Chair–CEO relationship, the Chair and the head of a committee should take the time to discuss formal and less visible boundaries and their respective concerns.

Committee work provides the opportunity for many contact points. I am a fan of companies organized like spider webs, with many contact points between players. Such an organization asks for awareness from the people involved. Just because it can lead to problems, the benefit of a broader interaction should not be lost.

BM: I believe in a web of connection, but it requires a high level of maturity and trust. If the management team is functioning well, they are communicating well, they are aligned on how decisions get made, and above all, they're not using that web of connection as a weapon to undermine decisions or undermine their peers, then plenty of connections are of great value.

Nomination Committee and Independence in Mind

Selecting the "right" new board members is fundamental to create a performing team, so the nomination committee has a dedicated subsection.

An excellent team requires recruiting the right people. This is universally true, especially so for the board of directors because, once installed, you will likely stay for some time. I question if the General Assembly is the decisive factor in board members' tendency to stay. It is hard to replace a top management position, but the psychological strain of tolerating a poor fit is far more prominent in a managerial position. On a board, the intensity of interaction is much less frequent and a board member has little direct impact on the rest of the organization, so the urgency to replace a weak board member is less immediate. If you know and like the person, the tendency to shy away from issues can lead to even greater tolerance. So, recruiting the right people onto the board is even more critical. A longer tenure also makes business sense: to provide value on a board, you need some time unless your unique experience means you can have an immediate effect.

Who should be in charge of recruitment? My interviewees did not dispute that the Chair plays a crucial role since he has to run the board. If the Chair is the head of the nomination committee, he should not be in that role when it comes to finding the Chair's successor or even in his succession planning.

> BM: One of the most dangerous things that an outgoing Chair can do is propose his successor. One can assume that the one proposed will not be better than the one who suggests him. He does not want it to be better. That is bad.

In the United Kingdom, the independent lead director is not allowed to become the new Chair and therefore is in a good position to lead the succession process of the Chair; he may also conduct the board review (see Chapter 11; for further discussion, see Dunne 2019).

It was also clear that the Chair should not dominate the recruitment process, the nomination process must be structured, and it must allow fresh and diverse forces to be brought in. Many companies involve executive search companies, increasing the likelihood of a fairer process and a broader field of candidates. Search companies have experience but also self-interest and tend to be risk averse; it is far easier to provide a list of known candidates with a proven track record as managers. Whether they fit as board members for that specific company is a different story. Search companies usually have little access to the boardroom or to the (unconscious) dynamics revealed in board meetings, which is essential to form an opinion on the profile needed. With a Chair leading the process, even a structured approach with an executive search company contains the inherent risk that old buddies are proposed. Once presented through such a process, it is tough to raise doubts about or have a challenging interview with such a person. Happy the companies where the Chair is fully aware of those pitfalls.

BM: If I choose colleagues from the Lions Club, I don't get the best candidates; then I end up with collegiate people, but that does not help.

BM: I declined some excellent friends because I saw that they would simply follow my lead and add nothing critical.

The quantitative part of my INSEAD thesis (Sieber 2019a) also provided a convincing result. Choosing your *existing* buddies to join you risks a silent board; out of loyalty, such a board member will tend to be quiet in moments that matter. However, *getting to know each other while on the board* provides more voice behavior (see earlier in this chapter).

Relying on external companies in no way precludes the discussion of what profile for a new face is needed on the board. I use the word profile not just regarding technical skills; cultural aspects are equally important, if not more so, but are often only considered to the extent of having a good feeling about somebody.

BM: In addition to the technical skills and the previously defined requirements, I was conscientious about ensuring that the board works, that is, those people like each other. This is certainly not a legal definition, not a scientific thing, but a board that gets along with each other. I was on boards where you left after the meeting, and you didn't care about what the others were doing. You were emotionally not engaged. Of course, the question of chumminess comes up quickly, but I didn't mean that; I meant that people like each other and have a certain interest in each other.

Listening to the gut is essential, but that alone will lead to a homogenous board with fewer debates; it is common knowledge that you feel more at ease with people similar to yourself.

An area that does not get the necessary attention but is, in my opinion, crucial for an active board and a strong team is the question of the *independence of mind*. Extensive research about independence stresses formal factors like tenure, gender, and management independence, thereby failing to consider that board members are human beings. Several board members were critical of the formal criteria, which do not reflect the real dimension of independence of mind.

BM: Somebody can be very independent and at the same time be in significant breach of formal independence criteria, and vice versa.

Everybody agreed that independence is the primary prerequisite for having an open dialogue within a board and should be tested thoroughly in the selection process. Many board members described "independence" as an attitude in which one is ready to leave the board at any point:

BM: You have to be able and willing to quit at any time.

BM: A genuinely independent member should be ready from the first meeting to state different opinions and as a result of this risk losing his/her mandate.

BM: If my opinion had no effect over time and were not listened to, then it would be time to leave the board—not because it was a waste of time, but because it would be purgatory.

BM: I have left boards, but it always felt like a personal failure. I could not convince the others. It hurts long-term relationships. Okay, you win a bit of self-esteem, but overall, it is an apparent and painful loss.

BM: You have to be ready to suffer personal disadvantages, irrespective of type (financial, social [prestige], and relational losses).

Let's have a look at quotes about those losses linked to the three kinds of independence:

Financial Independence

> *BM: I experienced that members were concerned about safeguarding a significant income source and added nothing critical. Let's be honest—for a few meetings—we are paid too much. Others have to work hard to get paid. Paying significantly less would help at least to be less dependent financially.*

> *BM: Even if you are rich, in my experience, it hurts nevertheless to lose a certain amount.*

> *BM: Board members are also homo economicus, and they are cautious about annoying the Chair who provides the food.*

Social Independence (Prestige)

> *BM: Those who need it out of ego motives and those who have nothing else to do have to be avoided.*

> *BM: Nonfinancial motives play a considerable role. I have many talks with colleagues who complain that you are nobody after you are out; you don't get invited to things anymore, your prestige is gone. Therefore, it is clear that you cling to your position, especially toward the end of a long and successful career, which does not help your independence of mind.*

Relationship Independence

From my quantitative INSEAD (Sieber 2019a) results, protecting relationships is a critical motive for board members to remain silent. One quote from many:

> *BM: One does not want to challenge the Chair because one feels the need to be loyal to him; he was responsible that I got selected; if I knew him previously because we are friends or have similar social connections, that makes it even harder to speak up.*

Boards are well advised to be cautious about new board members who have close or long-standing social ties to the Chair and should delve into the question of independence during the selection process.

> *BM: It is essential to check the independence of mind in the selection process; board processes are less rigorous than management selection processes. You don't dare to ask tough questions because the potential new board member has a lot of prestige.*

> *BM: We avoid tough questions about the person and talk about the business experience and former successes.*

Some Chairs said that they tried to assess the *independence of mind* during the selection process. It's a complicated issue to address, which many board members do not feel empowered to tackle. The easy way out is to avoid it altogether. However, one Chair said:

> *BM: I talk in the interview process about what kind of human being is sitting opposite me; we talk about childhood; how did you grow up? I try to understand if somebody is down to earth and has enough self-esteem to contradict [me].*

Another Chair stressed the wrong focus:

> *BM: We look too much for industrial sector skills (something we can show to the public) and underestimate leadership quality, which is much harder to get a grip on.*

To summarize: financial independence was considered essential but hard to achieve fully. Furthermore, focusing on this "*makes it more diffi-cult to give newcomers a chance because they are financially often less inde-pendent, which is a shame*" (BM). Without financial independence, it is harder to be independent, or as one *BM* stated: "*You are not independent if you are not financially independent (whether subjectively or objectively does not matter).*"

> *BM: However, compensation is often overrated; the feeling of being sent home and not being needed, not being included, the social loss*

can hurt more and prevent [them] from speaking up and is under-estimated.

And finally, the "wrong kind" of loyalty—an attitude of feeling "obliged" to the Chair instead of the company—can keep board members silent.

I close this section with a memorable quote that gives rise to hope:

BM: Independence of mind is not God-given. The same people can function under different leadership differently, which shows the Chair's importance.

This quote shows the overall importance of the Chair for board culture. The selection of new board members is crucial for every board and indicates if the board is a team or if the Chair dominates.

I do not favor the entire delegation of responsibilities to the nomination committee. In particular, close cooperation between the nomination committee and the whole board is essential in this area. The feeling of inclusion is fundamental here, and the focus on the new board member's personality (independence of mind) should have prominence. Board members should be explicitly encouraged to ask critical questions during the interview process. While enormous progress has been made in recruiting boards, the gap in how companies act in this area is vast. Overall, boards should focus more on the candidate's personality and involve the entire board in the recruitment process where needed.

Between Meetings

In the period between board meetings, you will interact with management, several board members, and the outside world. In all those interactions, you can display the essential attitude I've described.

Some Chairs regularly have follow-up calls with board members after the meeting:

BM: I circle around with crucial members to determine whether they felt the board meeting was productive, transparent, and honest.

Others call individual board members when they sense that something was off in the meeting:

BM: If I sense that something felt wrong, I do not let that fester and call the board member; relationships can be fragile, and I think trust is essential. Independent of how experienced a board member is, sometimes they just sort of give up during a discussion if they don't feel it's going to make a difference or if they think they're sort of losing a battle. They don't want to use up their "political currency of influence" for a nuance. But talking to the board member later shows that you care, enforce trust, and bond.

While calling individual board members after the meetings shows that you care and can occasionally be appropriate, it may exclude the others. Joint reflections after the meeting should minimize the need for such calls.

Some Chairs write to the board members between the meetings, without management being involved. I like the idea that sharing the information comes from the Chair and not from the management and is, therefore, less polished. It shows an inclusive attitude and balances the information asymmetry between the Chair and the board. It also shows what is essential for the Chair and stimulus to ask pointed questions regarding specific issues, such as strategy. Most boards complain that they spend too much time discussing the past instead of strategic topics (foresight) and want fewer presentations and more discussion (Beatty 2012). If you're going to talk about strategy seriously, you have to be ready to invest time in the company's challenges.

Board members should not put their thinking cap aside upon leaving the boardroom, so inviting views between meetings demonstrates that there is more expected than showing up once a quarter. You can also take the opportunity to ask your board members if they have any topics for future board meetings, helping them to feel included and take ownership, rather than just consume what is handed to them.

The time between the meetings is naturally where you have more extensive one-to-ones to board members:

BM: As Chair, you have to talk to each member for about an hour every six months. Then they "puke" from whatever disturbs them and keeps them busy. There's a lot if you have good people.

BM: I have two calls with each board member each year. I call them check-in calls without specific agenda. You hear a lot, and our board review shows that board members highly appreciate those calls.

BM: As Chair, I have a meeting with each board member twice a year. I am open-minded but, conversely, I expect the same from these people, and I also ask what I can improve in my work, preparation, which helps them, and vice versa. Learning from each other is essential.

Each board member has a unique experience, frames, and filters through which they perceive the world (Beatty 2012), and the task as a Chair is to extract the richness from this diversity of views. These talks are a means to learn, show appreciation, cover topics that are not relevant for the entire board, and get to know each other better. I would take time outside of a business setting once a year to get deeper professionally and personally.

Finally, a point needing delicate handling: let's say that the next meeting agenda has been prepared, board members have had a chance to voice a concern or wish, and the documents are sent out. As Chair of the board or a committee head, a board member calls you before the meeting to let you know something meaningful.

BM: But then some express a critical issue before the meeting, which I find okay in case of doubt because then it is at least conveyed. The Chair is aware of this and can also bring this in himself (not XY told me), but in the sense that this is a critical argument, I know one on the board is concerned about it.

Generally, as Chair, you should resist the temptation to invite board members to call you in advance—it should be the exception, not the rule, as stated by Beatty (2012); if somebody calls and tells you something, you can ask if they are willing to share that concern in the board meeting. The more you generate an attitude that sensitive topics are on the table, the more the board will act and feel like a team.

In any case, try to avoid having the meeting itself be only a friendly nod toward what has been decided beforehand in the "dark" chambers.

On the other hand, if a board member has a strong feeling about something and knows that it is crucial for the Chair or the CEO, it can be appropriate to tell them in advance that the member will bring those concerns into the meeting so that the Chair is not caught off-guard.

Finally, how such issues are handled should not be left in the dark. Addressing such a topic in a reflection session shows that you are willing to listen, reflect, and consider options. Combining your reflective personality with common sense will reveal the appropriate behavior in each case.

CHAPTER 6

The Chair's Interaction With the CEO

Communication must be HOT. Honest, Open and Two-way.
—Dan Oswald

The most important thing in communication is hearing what isn't said.

—Peter F. Drucker

Introduction

The relationship between the Chair and the CEO is the most important within a company. While the CEO runs the show, the Chair, with his board, selects and supervises the CEO and decides upon her remuneration (in some countries, subject to the General Assembly's approval). Whether the Chair or the entire board is the CEO's boss is disputed in literature and practice. In my opinion, without diminishing the board's role, it is the Chair because a body of many can't fulfill the specific tasks I focus on here. Being a trusted sparring partner, displaying a coaching attitude and setting boundaries are inherently part of a one-to-one relationship.

BM: If the tandem of Chair and CEO doesn't work, it's a disaster for the company.

BM: If the Chair and the CEO are not aligned, that can lead to a split board and a split senior management team. And what happens is then the entire organization becomes split.

BM: The most important thing is alignment between Chair and CEO. This does not mean that there's no challenge and there's no independence of the viewpoints. But when you have an unhealthy misalignment between the Chair's thinking and the CEO's thinking, that's very difficult.

BM: Speaking about alignment, one of my favorite analogies is from the movie "Finding Nemo." There's one scene where all the fish swim together downwards and manage to escape the fishing net. You get incredible power when you have an aligned organization, and all the directional energy is pointing in one principal direction.

BM: So, when you have two of the most senior people in the organization unable to converse, nothing good can come from it. The Chair and the CEO do not always have to agree, but they need mutual respect to have an open and honest conversation about issues. You can agree to disagree, but if you disagree, you still agree to commit to whatever solution is finally put on the table. Otherwise, the organization falls apart and what ends up happening is that, frankly, nothing happens, and when nothing happens and everyone else is moving forward, you fall behind.

BM: If there is friction, the impression must never be created that the two cannot work together.

BM: I had a very challenging relationship with my Chair. And I got to the point where I didn't want to debate anymore, and finally, I quit. I promised myself that I would act differently in the companies I am chairing. My job is not to run the company. My job is to make sure that management thinks through all the issues that are raised by my board and my board members help management to come up with a strategy that is well considered through, and that might reflect a broader set of expertise that may be the management team alone would not possess on their own. If a CEO ignores any input, is unwilling to change, and has no good reason not to listen, then quite simply, it's time to change the CEO.

The quotes ask for the necessary alignment and challenge between these positions, both accompanied by power and prestige. Past successes; current position; personalities; personal environment; pressure from the capital market; media attention; the search for success; the need for recognition: these are all reasons why we should not assume that the Chair and CEO will quickly work out their relationship. Too often, it doesn't.

I have formulated some guiding principles of do's and don'ts for a high-functioning relationship. Mainly, I have written from a Chair perspective, but I also reflect on how CEOs would like to see their ideal Chair.

Hypothetical Example

A compliance issue in a subsidiary with the potential to hurt the company pops up, mainly on the reputational front. The CEO has just received the information and much is still unclear. She hesitates to inform the Chair but decides—against natural reflex—to wait until the picture is clearer to notify him. The subsidiary is not core, and the CEO has thought about selling it but has not yet discussed it with the Chair. The Chair has a long-lasting emotional relationship with the subsidiary because he managed its turnaround in his early years. The Chair has a gut feeling that the focus has been recently on innovation and empowering culture, while the importance of stability and adherence to process does not seem to have had the necessary attention.

When the CEO shares the potentially troublesome issue, the Chair is disappointed and angry. He says that it doesn't surprise him since compliance issues recently haven't had the attention necessary. The CEO is disgruntled with his reaction because the Chair raises his pet topic, which she considers unfair. The Chair has not honored that she chose to share information promptly without having the whole picture. She reacts by breaking the news that she has been thinking about selling the noncore company anyway. The Chair is hurt but does not share why. Instead, he tells the CEO that he will mandate the internal audit department to perform a special compliance audit in the respective subsidiary. Later he informs the board about what happened and receives widespread validation for his decisive intervention.

At the end of this chapter, I will return to this exchange and review how those two could have reacted instead.

Do's and Don'ts

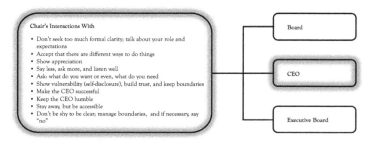

Figure 6.1 Chair's interaction with the CEO

Don't Seek Too Much Formal Clarity; Talk About Your Role and Expectations

While the law describes the allocation of responsibilities and by-laws lay it out in more detail specific to companies, I will make a provocative statement as a former general counsel. The time invested in by-laws is often not worth the effort or resources. Business and daily life realities are too complicated to be adequately captured in full detail in formal documents.

> BM: *You can't describe who does what on 30 pages; basically, there has to be room on the back of an envelope.*

My philosophy is: less is more. Reduce to the minimum, be more principle-based than rule-based. I refer here specifically to the responsibilities of the Chair and the CEO. The fewer people involved, the less necessary, and the shorter the rules should be.

There is no doubt that a company has to comply with all regulations; while minimizing the company's (and, to a certain extent, personal) risk is more than legitimate, it needs to be balanced with seeking opportunities for the company.

> BM: *The focus on rules and regulation and minimizing risks got so heavy over the last decade that we miss time to discuss opportunities.*

Experience has taught me that the wish for rules and clarity at the top often has a much more personal motivation. People may *consciously* stress the need for clarity and therefore argue for more formal rules, while *unconsciously,* there is a desire for demarcation. I used to say that clarity seekers are often "garden thinkers": *this is my garden to play in, and that is yours. As long as we respect this, we will get along perfectly.*

One of the hottest business topics is the need for greater collaboration (see also Edmondson 2012). I am convinced that collaboration has more to do with mindset than with rules. Rules sometimes lead to less consideration of what could make sense in a specific situation and damage collaboration.

My general view—applied to the Chair–CEO relationship—is confirmed by new research by Morais, Kakabadse, and Kakabadse (2018). They conclude that boundaries should be relatively flexible, not static, and demand continuously adapted according to circumstance. Clearer boundaries may be easier for accountability but seem less appropriate in facing increasingly dynamic challenges in the business environment.

Disputing an issue by referring to internal rules can be a sign that something fundamental is missing. Regardless of how many written rules you may produce, an essential ingredient is that both people consider the interests and needs of the other person and talk about them. This attitude is fundamental to giving the interests of the company the highest priority.

A former CEO and now board member said:

> BM: *Before I finally decided to take the job, I had a very long, intense and extremely open conversation with the Chair about our respective understanding of the complementary roles and responsibilities. It was the essential foundation stone for our successful relationship later on.*

According to Covey (2020), most *relationship difficulties are rooted in conflicting role understanding and expectations.* Taking your time and talking about roles and expectations usually pays off later. Don't take too much for granted and rely on formal clarity; be flexible, reevaluate from time to time, and adjust when necessary.

Accept That There Are Different Ways to Do Things

People are different; they have different ways of doing things. As Peter Drucker (2010) states, your approach is as individualistic as you are. And this is also true for the relationship between the Chair and the CEO. If you want a strong CEO, then you have to let her do her job.

> BM: *The Chair may be very reserved in the factual issues, which defuses many areas of conflict; what is decisive, even if he has the most profound conviction to be right, is that he can accept rationally and emotionally that the CEO may have different opinions, which can also lead to success.*

One board member relates a conversation between a Chair and a CEO:

> BM: *I had a fundamental difference of opinion with my CEO about a leader of one of our subsidiaries. I didn't think that he had the capability and the ambition to improve the results. I flagged it to my CEO and said: "I don't believe that he should be around next year."*

> CEO: *"I know he's not the best, but from a management team perspective, he is essential. I'll make sure that I have an extra focus to improve the results of that subsidiary."*

> BM: *"Then you're doing his job for him. You validated my point!"*

> CEO: *"I do not disagree entirely with your point, but I still think it's right at this moment that he is staying for the stability and team dynamics."*

> BM: *I did not force the issue and gave the CEO the benefit of the doubt that she would turn things around, and she did. My point is that I strongly challenged the CEO, but I also respected the arguments and the boundaries of the roles of a CEO versus a Chair. You have to give the CEO the responsibility to put together her team except when there is a very dramatic difference of opinion.*

As a Chair, challenge the CEO but avoid putting your discretion and judgment above hers.

> BM: *Hopefully, I generally make the right decisions regarding how far to push a point and understand the boundaries of the roles of a CEO versus a Chair. The Chair's job is to work with the board to ensure that you have the right CEO and provide the right environment for the CEO.*

Such an attitude needs self-restraint and generosity to accept different viewpoints. However, if fundamental value issues are concerned, tolerance should be minimal, and neither should be shy in addressing them. But the message is: if you want a strong CEO for the business, you cannot wish for a weak CEO in her dealings with you.

Show Appreciation

When a CEO suffered from harsh treatment by the Chair or a scathing article in the media, I often heard statements at my regular tennis group that missed the point, such as, "Her suffering is compensated by the paycheck." All human beings need recognition and appreciation. At the top, you often get "false" recognition and appreciation from people who try to please you. Genuine appreciation is a scarce commodity, especially from those who matter the most.

I have intentionally chosen the word "appreciation" and not "recognition." Recognition is appropriate and necessary when earned and deserved, but it is performance based and, therefore, conditional to success. Appreciation acknowledges the person rather than being linked to a specific accomplishment. Appreciation should stay even if you suffered a loss. It is more profound, and it is more impactful because it is about you as an individual. "In simple terms, recognition is about what people do; appreciation is about who they are" (Robbins 2019).

I liked the following description of a CEO's ideal Chair:

> *BM: Someone who is highly critical and challenging when things are going very well and highly supportive when things are not going the way we all want them to go.*

In the business world, we are less practiced at expressing appreciation.

> *BM: I am an analytical person. I hardly ever praise. I don't use praise to achieve anything.*

> *BM: I hardly praise; once you start, you can't stop.*

Robbins (2019) mentions a few elementary guidelines in showing appreciation. Listen genuinely; tell people what you value about them, and do a check-in which is a proper check-in. Rather than just starting right away with the topic of the meeting, ask the person what is on their mind, how they are feeling. We often run from one session to the other, physically present but mentally still absorbed with the previous one. One of my former direct reports used check-ins when we had our one-to-one, and I learned to appreciate them. Showing appreciation helps the recipient's self-esteem and builds your relationship, allowing the recipient to stay focused on what matters.

Insufficient appreciation from the Chair can make a CEO worry about her safety. Our brains scan our environment five times a second to ask: Is it safe here? When the brain senses danger, we go into a fight-or-flight response, also called the "amygdala hijack." Not a place where you want your CEO to be because she will be less able *to engage her conscious brain* (Stanier 2016).

Being questioned affects our motivational need system, which makes us behave the way we do. One of these fundamental needs is attachment, as previously described. If this need is poorly met, it affects self-esteem. Do I belong to this company? Is my contribution still valued? If you are anxious and preoccupied, you lose your concern for fellow workers and customers. It is called *self-absorption* (Bridges, 152) and certainly doesn't help the company's well-being. Sufficient appreciation helps the CEO focus on her real task and worry less about how the Chair evaluates her. It's naïve to believe that a paycheck compensates for suffering because that suffering can have effects that hurt the CEO's well-being and the entire group.

It follows that the Chair, leaving center stage to the CEO and being more the discrete, less visible guide, also needs enough appreciation. This statement is true for everybody but may sound hollow applied to a Chair or CEO. But, while the business world would make great efforts to deny it, insufficient appreciation for a Chair or a CEO is often the root cause of dysfunctional behavior, with severe consequences. Both Chair and CEO are well advised to be generous in showing appreciation—explicitly or implicitly.

Say Less, Ask More, and Listen Well

I have taken several coaching courses and read many coaching books. My favorite—easy to read and understand—is *The Coaching Habit: Say*

Less, Ask More, and Change the Way You Lead Forever by Michael Bungay Stanier (2016). In my last years in management, I tried to learn this habit and had plenty of encouragement to continue with it. Easy to read does not necessarily mean easy to apply. As managers, we are trained, and it is expected to provide advice under a time constraint. Changing our habits takes significant effort and continuous repetition.

Stanier (2016, p. 6) claims that "the seemingly simple behavior of giving a little less advice and asking a few more questions is surprisingly difficult. … You might be less certain whether you're useful, the conversation can feel slower, and you might feel like you have somewhat lost control of the conversation (and indeed you have. That's called "empowering")."

Stanier (2016) describes what a great coach or leader should do. Besides asking one question at a time and avoiding "why questions," which often triggers a defensive reaction, he mentions seven essential questions:

1. What's on your mind? *It is a great opener that leaves autonomy to make choices to the addressee. It delivers trust.*
2. And what else? *A powerful question that works against the advice monster. It creates new possibilities.*
3. What is the real challenge here for you? *It allows us to focus on the real, not the first, problem.*
4. What do you want? *This is the foundation question (see next to do's in that subchapter).*
5. How can I help? *This is a lazy question that sharpens the request without leaping into action.*
6. If you are saying "Yes" to this, what are you saying "No" to? *The "no" helps you understand the decision and puts the spotlight on the "yes."*
7. What was the most useful for you? *That is the learning question. You show that you are willing to learn.*

Since the Chair has a coaching role toward the CEO, this coaching attitude is of utmost importance for the Chair function.

BM: As a CEO, you are often lonely and have to be strong at all times—toward all employees, your team, and even more so with cus-

tomers and third-party stakeholders. You need someone as a sparring partner—if the Chair can take on this role, it is immensely helpful.

A coaching attitude demands a listening attitude, keeping your thoughts to yourself and your attention on the CEO's turf. Asking is excellent, but what you ask and in which order makes a difference.

I had an interesting exchange with a former CEO who was in the process of taking a Chair position. He pointed out that he will always try to start the CEO's conversation by asking how he can help (Stanier's question number 5, mentioned earlier) to prevent giving advice immediately. I asked him what this question could trigger with the CEO. The former CEO was first a bit puzzled and quiet, and then he finally said:

BM: I put myself in the center. The CEO has to think about how I could help; instead, she should be placed in a position where she shares what is on her mind, not be pushed into thinking about how I could help her.

I was proud that I had not leaped into the management habit to say right away what I thought instead of triggering his insight with a simple question. If the CEO cannot think quickly about something the Chair could help with, the Chair is disappointed or will tell her how he can help. "How can I help?" is an excellent question, but—as the example shows—there is a subtle, essential difference in starting a dialogue by asking "what is on your mind" instead of "how can I help?"

Try to meet the CEO where she is and listen to what she has to tell you. A great listener can clarify the speaker's thought processes. I'm sure you have experienced a situation where you were just listening, and suddenly the speaker had an "aha" moment. Such a listening attitude demands that *you master your ego and quiet your voice* (Dignan 2019). Listening gets even harder when you are in a leadership position because people tend to defer to authority; this is why so many senior leaders are poor listeners and do most of the talking anytime they are in the room. Keltner (2016) coined the term "the power paradox" to describe how leaders gain influence through empathy but lose those skills as they gain influence and power.

Great listening means hearing the words and listening to the voice (tone, pace, volume) and watching body language (gestures, facial expressions, posture). We have all had situations where we talked to someone and later had a very different understanding of what they wanted to express. Covey (2020) states of the four communication forms—reading, writing, speaking, and listening—that, in contrast to the first three, we are not trained in listening.

In a critical project in my younger years, my boss had a very different understanding of what his boss wanted us to do. I said to my boss: *independent from your boss's exact words, it was evident to me what he wanted.* But my boss was not convinced, so he wanted to go back for clarification. His boss's reaction should have been *thanks for coming back to get clarification.* Instead, he said: *Do you think that I was drunk when I gave you that task?*

Later on, it became apparent that my boss did not like the project's direction at all. He listened with his frame which clouded his understanding.

> *BM: I think the most brilliant of the executives or Chairs are the ones that realize they're not always right. Therefore, they listen very carefully and hear potential counterpoints instead of listening to get confirmation.*

"Say less, ask more, and listen well" are crucial habits for each leader, especially the Chair.

Ask: What Do You Want or Even What Do You Need?

I mentioned that Chair and CEO should talk about roles and expectations. In western culture, especially in countries with a strong "explicit culture" like the United States or Germany, making expectations explicit is common (Meyer 2014). However, it's one thing to be clear and communicate your expectations explicitly; it's a different matter altogether to be willing to ask that of another person. By doing so, you give up a degree of control: you may hear unwelcome issues that you have to digest. The heart of Stanier's book is the foundational question: *What do you want?* Often, we do not address what we want, address it too nebulously, or address it, but the addressee's confirmation bias is so strong that we are not heard. Both parties to the conversation tend to assume they know what the other wants.

When in doubt, we shy away from tackling the open issue to avoid immediate disappointment or naïvely convince ourselves that the problem will work itself out somehow, a widespread behavior in top management circles, confirmed by my interviewees and Drucker (2010). He writes that most organizational issues derive from personality conflicts, which often arise because we don't talk about what is crucial for us. We do not know what is vital for others because we haven't asked and therefore haven't been told. Having asked, a common reaction we face is *thanks for asking, but why didn't you ask me earlier?*

> BM: *We had a constellation where both the Chair and the CEO had a lot of expertise. The Chair responded to data intuitively while the CEO responded analytically—basically, an excellent combination. However, the two communicated with each other poorly and did not make an effort to integrate their different ways of thinking to arrive at a common result. Many misunderstandings happened because they could not look from the other's perspective and did not ask for the other's perspective. A lot was unspoken. Accordingly, there were injuries on both sides; rather than resolution, more division occurred.*

> BM: *I had a very, very rich CEO. I assumed wrongly that the remuneration did not matter to him. And he did not need the money, but he cared about showing up in a magazine where CEOs' pay was published. That never crossed my mind. He would have happily given the money back to the company as long as he showed up in that magazine league table. That example shows that we should not merely presume, and it helps to get to know people; then, it is less likely such wrongful assumptions are made in the first place, and we are more inclined to ask and share what is essential for us. You should know what makes the other people tick.*

Those two examples are probably more common than we imagine. While "say less and ask more" should be a general habit that would help us all, it is no guarantee that all underlying topics are surfaced. Stanier makes the vital distinction between "want" and "need." Need is more profound. You are well advised to listen for underlying needs, like protection, understanding, affection, or identity. If the Chair says to the CEO: *I want you to do this*, the underlying message is maybe *I need you to do this because I feel uncomfortable doing it*. The need might be to protect himself from discomfort.

Can we go further and ask directly? I dare to say "yes." To quote Peter Drucker (2010): "If you don't ask, you may never know." The "want" question is probably more accessible since it's closer to a specific task and less deep; talking about "need" preferably takes place independent of a particular issue. Asking for something unrelated to an urgent matter provides time and space to have a wonderful conversation. What are your values? How do you react when you are hurt? What do I need to know about your strengths? How do you perform at your best? During my INSEAD education, we asked ourselves questions like:

- What makes you angry?
- What makes you happy?
- What makes you sad?

Later on, I tried this out with my management team. It was amazing what we learned about each other, although we had worked together for a long time. We felt a more robust group bond after that exercise.

Asking is essential, and it can build trust. It helps to understand. It helps to avoid misunderstandings. But one crucial thing is missing, which is vital to build trust and get honest answers. I wrote about it in Chapter 2: you have to share yourself too.

Show Vulnerability (Self-Disclosure), Build Trust, and Keep Boundaries

"To say what we want" can sound like a demand; to share a need goes deeper, but what we really should do is to *share a need with an explanation of why it is so vital* for us, providing a frame and a context. Here, we enter the field of sharing vulnerability (Brown 2018).

We have seen that we need both trust and to share ourselves to build a well-functioning relationship. A relationship built on trust prevents role constraints between the Chair and the CEO or removes them through open debate and collaboration. A high level of trust reduces tensions, anxieties, and defensiveness by confronting critical issues (e.g., Lewis 2000). In the view of my interviewees, trust was an undisputed ingredient for relationships to function well, while showing vulnerability caused a broad spectrum of reactions, from being a necessity to being unnecessary.

Showing vulnerability is not a behavior typically expected on the top floor. Nevertheless, I can include some quotes disclosing insecurities, showing emotions, and apologizing for being wrong. Such behavior can have a tremendous effect on others:

> BM: When you show feelings, you show passion. Too often people show themselves like robots and suppress feelings, which is terrible for everyone involved. They have a wall around them and inside is a fragile egg; I often feel sorry for these managers.

> BM: Showing your weaknesses makes you stronger. I have no inhibitions about that. I share all my feedback (numbers and verbatim) with my team; how can they observe me and support my learning if they don't know what I'm working on?

> BM: When I started as a CEO, I told my executive board team that they all know much more than I do. They were surprised about my statement, although I stated the obvious. In a way, I was saying that I need them, and they had not expected such a statement.

> BM: I was a bit harsh toward a board member and made an error in reasoning. Later, in the reflection session, I apologized, which was perceived very well by the entire board.

> BM: I frankly have no issue with showing vulnerability. I think that the most courageous executives are the ones that admit they're not perfect and they don't have all the answers and admit that they've made mistakes. It tends to open people's minds when the most potent people say: "Let's figure this out together." Genuinely, that's when I have the most fun when the team tries to solve a problem. That's when all the intellectual juices are flowing. Otherwise, you're doing something you've done before. And frankly, that's not as interesting.

A Chinese executive board member offered the most touching story:

BM: In a leadership workshop, we talked about our missions, our values, and even about our childhood. Honestly, I didn't believe in such exercises. At the end of our workshop, where everybody had to share, the new CEO sat down on the floor, crossed her legs, and said: "I am scared about me being the new CEO, and I have doubts about whether I deserve this promotion because I never got a college degree." Her showing vulnerability had a tremendous effect on all participants, and I vowed that I would do everything to make her successful as CEO. It also made it easier for me to show vulnerability later with my team; however, it is still tricky in the board team.

A Chair with a CEO history offered the following reflection, and I wondered if the attitude expressed is, in fact, not a very common one:

BM: I need the CEO to be transparent; it builds trust if a CEO can say that she does not know how to proceed; I even say she should show her vulnerability. Hearing myself speak, I wonder why I have trouble showing vulnerability. Is it my upbringing? Once, an important relationship on the board with a joint-venture partner turned sour because I could not address that I felt angry and hurt. Today, to my benefit, I address critical issues earlier by asking questions and, if appropriate, disclosing my feelings.

Several interviewees acknowledged that sharing vulnerability is something they had to learn:

BM: I had to learn to reveal something about myself as well.

Sharing vulnerability is not just sharing. It always needs intention, context, and boundaries. Brown (2018) writes, "vulnerability without boundaries is not vulnerability." It is a confession, desperation, or even manipulation.

Let's look at some examples of showing vulnerability: you have an important meeting, but you feel distracted because you have to wait for the doctor to call you about a diagnosis. Sharing your fear and explaining why you are distracted is sharing vulnerability.

Or something more directly business related: the company is in the process of hiring a person, someone the CEO is all in favor of. As a Chair, you feel rushed and had a terrible experience in the past with a similar process. It can make a difference if you share why you are hesitant about the process. If you don't, the CEO may misinterpret your hesitation: *Maybe, the Chair doesn't like the candidate, or is something else going on that I don't know?*

A final example is one of my interviewees, who shared something personal because it was related to an area where the company was not doing great, so it had the necessary intention and context.

> BM: *Integrating my work into my life and not the other way around is essential for me. Employee surveys in our organization show that we have to improve in the area of work–life balance. One day, I couldn't go on. I allowed myself to be vulnerable and gathered the courage to share it with my team and ask for help. This allowed all of us to share how we were managing ourselves. Since then, whenever I get an opportunity, I share my experience with a larger employee audience and, from the feedback I have got so far, this is touching many people and encouraging others to share their experience thus creating a psychologically safe work environment to be ourselves and ask for help when we are struggling more so during this COVID-19 pandemic period.*

Sharing vulnerability and keeping boundaries lead us to how close the Chair and CEO should get in their relationship. A majority of the interviewees believed that it was important not to limit their relationship with the CEO to business issues.

> BM: *We've known each other for a long time and sometimes meet privately. We also discuss things not directly related to the company, making it easier to include company topics. Chair and CEO must build up a relationship on a personal level, but this must not then become a consensus-oriented relationship where these two always have the same opinions, then it becomes dangerous; very resilient, substantive work*

should be more accessible with a personal relationship, so that nothing personal stands in the way of the substantive.

A more reserved attitude is expressed in the following:

BM: You need to know your CEO, which includes more personal things; it is vital to building trust, but it is professional trust; you should not be the CEO's friend. Therefore, I don't do private events with my CEO.

BM: I see that you need to understand the whole person or not just the business side of the person. But I don't want to get too close and so I would be thinking in all circumstances it's important that you know that you're going to have lunch or dinner with the CEO from time to time, but a business type of dinner rather than a social type of thing. If you start to get too close and go around to each other's houses, I worry that it could be drifting into a relationship that undermined the ability to challenge effectively because you're too close. It is a question of finding the right balance.

BM: Showing vulnerability is a little bit of a mess. Once you open it, it changes the relationship from a more business type to friendship. And Chair–CEO should not be best friends.

The main reason Chairs felt concerned about showing vulnerability was the fear of getting too close to the CEO (see the introduction as well). One Chair talked about a family-owned business and raved about the family's very personal style while managing to make a clear separation of business and private life, thereby keeping a very professional relationship.

Our cultural background certainly plays an important role, but even within the same region, differences are considerable; our natural inclination is the decisive factor in finding the right place for us between "proximity" and "distance" (see Chapter 3 about attachment style, especially the Riemann/Thomann Cross). Being aware of these preferences can help us find the right balance.

It is in the interest of the entire board that the Chair and the CEO get along well, but not that the relationship gets *too* friendly. The danger is that the others feel excluded and that the necessary checks and balances of independence disappear.

> *BM: Getting too close doesn't help the board as a team because the board will feel like outsiders and excluded.*

> *BM: I have seen one example where the Chair was way too close to the CEO and the rest of the board members felt left aside. They [the Chair and CEO] agreed on everything and were pushing in the same direction.*

> *BM: If the Chair and CEO are too close, the likelihood that the Chair fails to provide any brake to the CEO is more significant. I experienced such a constellation; the Chair was only the accelerator for the CEO, which is fine for many things but not okay for everything; you can't drive the car with just the accelerator.*

As in many areas in life, success is achieved in finding the right balance between showing vulnerability and setting boundaries; each person has to find their proper path, but we should be aware that our chosen path changes how we are perceived and how we build relationships.

With daring generalization, my interviews showed that the prototype of a person who had trouble showing vulnerability was older, male, and had a very prestigious job. Men often suppress emotions because we learn as boys not to cry and not to show weaknesses. According to a global research project of Zehnder (2018), CEOs generally expressed confidence with different behaviors; *showing emotions*, however, got twice as many "feeling uncomfortable" votes as *proposing radical new ideas which might feel risky* or more than a factor of three of the votes for "admitting own mistakes." I believe that showing vulnerability is a great strength that needs self-esteem and courage and enables us to connect. Without authentic connections, we suffer (see Chapter 2). I am convinced that many relationships would improve if we learned to show vulnerability. In an environment where it is not the normal observed behavior, you should start cautiously.

> *BM: I have had the experience that, as a woman, it is more acceptable to talk about feelings. Most of the time, this was key to success. If you don't open up and lead with your heart, the people will not go through the fire, show passion, and walk the extra mile!*

BM: I have done well to be myself, to show vulnerability before it really hurts when it is often too late and the damage has already been done.

Without sharing our vulnerability, we hide our true feelings; we don't connect and learn. We should operate from "self-awareness and not self-protection," as Brown (2018) states. If we are self-aware and choose to be consciously vulnerable, it will also be easier to handle boundary issues. I even believe that it is easier to address boundaries issues if you have a trusted and open relationship; such a relationship is more resilient and will allow you in addressing boundary issues with doing less harm as long as you honestly reflect upon your behavior and are ready to tackle a problem with somebody you like. Keep in mind that good professional relationships should help you, your environment, and above all the company; not addressing an issue because you are afraid of harming the relationship is putting the value of the relationship above the company's well-being; you can perhaps do this as the owner, but not as a board member or manager.

I believe that the whole business world would be a better place if we could make further progress in showing vulnerability.

BM: I was in a challenging situation. All the others had spoken, and nobody has asked me. Then I said that I would like to share how I feel, and I felt hurt. I did not get an immediate response, but several board members approached me after the meeting and expressed that my ability to show vulnerability was essential.

However, the interviews showed pretty clearly that it is not (yet) the norm to show vulnerability:

BM: It is not easy for me to be open and share that I am insecure. People expect that I have the answers and usually I do. Sometimes, my ego stands in my way; sometimes, it is fear of a loss of control over the communication.

It goes hand-in-hand that I sensed a reluctance to ask about the needs of others. Overall, the interviewees expressed readiness to act more openly, hoping that the other side will reciprocate, but not to talk more about individual needs and feelings.

We've all heard that actions speak louder than words. But that statement assumes that we know what is essential for the other party or that they know what is vital for us. As we have seen earlier, being ready for self-disclosure is necessary for teams and all relationships. Schein and Schein (2021, p. 78) argues that, especially in U.S. business culture, which is more task oriented than relationship oriented, people come together to get things done and little more. As a result, business relationships tend to be impersonal. "This often leads to a professional relationship that may involve an implicit effort by the relevant parties to actively avoid personal involvement with each other; even favoring professional distance as the best path to task accomplishment."

I was involved in a merger in Brazil, which progressed slowly at first because the more relationship-oriented Brazilians did not develop trusted relationships with task-oriented U.S. Americans. My assumption, and indeed hope, is that increasing diversity in business, and the growing complexity of tasks calling for more collaboration, will demand more profound and personal relationships.

Make the CEO Successful

If you were there when the CEO was elected, you played an essential role in choosing her. Now is the time to support her so that (hopefully) you can enjoy the company's success.

Real Example

I was on a board of directors characterized by its binational structure. The board of directors had precisely the same number of members from two countries. While the Chair was from country X, the CEO was from Y. Such a constellation is quite common after a merger of equals. However, the dual structure also continued at the management level. Next to the CEO was a "deputy CEO" from the other country. This "deputy CEO" (country X) claimed to have a direct line to the

Chair (country X) and, worse, most of the board members of country X strongly supported that view. There were often situations where the CEO requested something during a board meeting, and the "deputy CEO" expressed a dissenting opinion. Ultimately, such an organization gives the board control and power, but the CEO can hardly lead. Consciously accepting such a constellation means that you as a board put your power above the company's success.

Together with a board peer from the other country, we were asked to develop a proposal that considered the dual country structure but let the CEO lead her team.

While this example may be extreme, the problem described occurs more than we might think. It is probably less structural and more about how a company makes important decisions. For example, if the Chair asks for a unanimous decision from the executive board, he weakens the CEO. As alluring it may seem to strengthen your position and influence as a Chair, don't fall into this trap. Support the CEO for the best of the company, which means helping her with her team to arrive at a good decision and not maximize your influence. This may be counterintuitive, so it needs reflective behavior from the Chair.

Restraining yourself and focusing on strengthening and supporting the CEO is a great starting point. It is about finding the right balance, in this case, between supporting your CEO and not losing the confidence of your board. It may end up that your board members perceive you to be an arm of the CEO:

BM: My board members don't perceive me as independent; they see me too aligned with the CEO and sometimes get pretty frustrated. Sometimes, I feel that some board members believe that I am just following the CEO's opinion.

"Make the CEO successful" is a question of attitude. It is not about strengthening your position; it is honestly thinking about how you can best support the CEO. She has a challenging job and needs your support, which includes challenging her, nudging her sometimes, comforting her, shielding her, and providing feedback. According to a global report by Zehnder (2018), only about a third of the Chairs provide feedback to the CEO, underlining how isolating a CEO's position can be. The report concludes that boards and Chairs are not sufficiently supportive of the CEO.

What a CEO needs depends heavily on her personality and circumstances; as a Chair, you have to be adaptive in how you interact with her; sometimes you are almost not needed.

BM: I genuinely believe that we all should learn and develop. Yes, my job as a Chair includes working with my top management with a coaching attitude. Feedback needs to factor in the personality type of the individual you're speaking to. One is a high performer and high demander; he is probably one of the most abrasive executives I've had the pleasure of working with. He runs desert marathons and has difficulty understanding why his team or colleagues don't run as hard. And then, I have another CEO who is very reserved and introverted by nature. I can't be as direct and harsh with him as with the marathon guy.

Keep the CEO Humble

Humility is undoubtedly an attitude that should be desirable in Chair and CEO (see also Chapter 3 for the essential personality traits of a Chair). Research makes it clear that humble leaders improve a company's performance because they create a more collaborative environment (Lambrechts, Bouwen, Grieten, Huybrechts, and Schein and Schein 2021; for further references, see Mayo 2018, pp. 43–44). Companies today have fewer hierarchies, structures, and boundaries. When everybody calls for agility, the collaboration within teams and between them is crucial for tomorrow's success; collaboration is essential, and collaboration calls for humility.

Humble leaders have a balanced view of themselves. They see their strengths and development areas and have a strong appreciation for the contributions of others. They are open to new ideas and feedback. A humble CEO leads to a more humble organization because managers and employees follow their leaders' attitudes.

Staying humble calls for an attitude of self-awareness and self-reflection to connect your personal development and the well-being of the organization. When a leader puts the organization's needs first, the leader gains respect and, in turn, is likely to continue to put the organization first (Quinn 2005).

As a Chair, you should be humble yourself and, in particular, watch out that your CEO stays humble; as a Chair, you probably have the most significant influence and leverage over the CEO.

It was surprising that some Chairs had a fatalistic view of the CEO: *either it works or doesn't*. If you missed harmful traits in the hiring process (Lencioni 2016), it is tough to change things later. Asked what Chairs could have done differently, the typical answer was to pull the trigger earlier.

> *BM: I should have pulled the ripcord earlier. CEOs are like generals on the battlefield; they can be proud and have charisma, but usually, there is a lack of wisdom when this quality becomes too dense; the feeling dominates that the organization is there for the CEO and not the other way around. CEOs fail not because of technical skills but because of character issues; they become arrogant and lie when necessary. Good proposals from the company are not understood. CEOs who are on the wrong track will not change for the better; as a Chair, don't delude yourself. With total modesty, a Chair must have the absolute claim to power to draw the line and kick the CEO out.*

But some Chairs felt lonely in dealing with a flawed CEO (see Chapter 5 about talking about your relationship with the CEO with the board).

> *BM: The weeds may grow slowly at first, and the board may not want to see them at all as long as the numbers are correct. But suddenly the lawn is full of weeds, and then there is only the goodbye.*

I may be naïve, but I believe that a lot is possible in a relationship if issues are addressed early on. But you need to have an attitude of not shying away from unpleasant matters.

> *BM: It is an absolute necessity to tackle personal issues early on— always with respect—before they grow above your head.*

BM: When I am in a "safe" space, I am used to speaking my mind and showing how I feel. I don't like to keep baggage because if you forgive, you're not a prisoner to the bitterness that comes with unforgiveness, so I prefer clarifying things, letting go, and moving on, hoping that the other person is also moving on.

Being values minded and having good judgment helps form an opinion on what behavior needs to be addressed. I liked the courageous intervention of one female board member:

BM: The CEO used—in my opinion—very abrasive language in a board meeting, and nobody reacted. After the board meeting, a few board members stayed around, so I asked them if I was too sensitive but did not appreciate the CEO's language. The board members were confirming my view and encouraged me to talk to the Chair. Since I am the head of the people's committee, I also felt responsible. So, I called the Chair, who agreed that we need to tell the CEO that his language was unacceptable, and he needs to be aware of how he communicates and comes across.

Precisely what the CEO said is not important. The point is that the board member did not look away; she addressed the wrong behavior.

Digression: Narcissistic Leaders

Narcissism is often described as being the opposite of humility. Staying humble as you step up the corporate ladder is a challenge, leading many to fall into the trap of narcissism. According to Kets de Vries (2014b), pathological narcissism is the most frequently found dysfunction at senior levels. In organizational psychology, narcissism is defined as a personality trait entailing a grandiose sense of the self, paired with self-affirmative strategies and disregard for others. It exists in all individuals to varying degrees (Braun 2017). Thanks to a strong sense of entitlement, becoming impatient or angry is a typical trait of such individuals when they don't receive the special treatment they believe they deserve. Not recognizing others' feelings and needs (low empathy), handling criticism poorly, becoming hurt easily, over-reacting, and defensiveness are characteristics of narcissistic behavior (Kets de Vries 2017). Dealing with leadership narcissism is tough if the pathological leadership behavior comes from the very top of the organization or the CEO herself and instills a culture of silence.

Narcissistic leaders seem confident, but that confidence masks deep vulnerability. Although they give off an impression of having high self-esteem, they are "troubled by a deep sense of insecurity" and put in a "heroic effort to compensate for their profound vulnerability" (Kets de Vries 2017). Working with them becomes challenging. To establish a relationship, you should first convey empathy and respect, acknowledging their need to be recognized. Becoming motivated to change will need to be driven by realizing that doing so might help them achieve their own goals and ambitions (Kets de Vries 2014a). For further strategies for dealing with leaders perceived as narcissistic, see Pomin (2019).

What I quoted here is pathological narcissism. According to Kets de Vries (2004), a healthy dose of narcissism is necessary to survive since "assertiveness, self-confidence, tenacity, and creativity just can't exist without it." For significant pros and the inevitable cons of narcissistic leaders, see Maccoby (2004).

We should be cautious in labeling somebody narcissistic. Com-panies seem to have an appetite for leaders exhibiting many of the characteristics of narcissists, assuming leadership positions require those traits (Braun 2017; Kets de Vries 2017) or as Mayo (2018) puts it: "If humble leaders make better leaders, why do we fall for charismatic narcissists?" Research suggests that narcissistic lead-ers radiate an image of a prototypically effective leader. They know how to attract attention, enjoy the spotlight, and appear convincing. It often takes time to realize the darker side: reducing information exchange among teams and being unsupportive of collaboration. Per-sonality assessments are poor at seeing behind the curtain; for internal recruitment, employees are an underutilized tool, being well placed to spot narcissistic tendencies.

While narcissism is perceived as unfavorable, charisma is perceived as positive. We like to be surrounded by charismatic people who radiate energy and a positive attitude. Charismatic leaders tend to be narcissistic; charisma depends heavily on followers' perception and context (Avery 2004). I like Mayo's statement (2018) that humble leaders can also be charismatic. Researchers classify charismatic leaders as negative or positive by the orientation toward pursuing their self-interest goals (personalized charisma) versus those of their groups (socialized charisma). The latter can also have a hero aura but show low authoritarianism and high interest in collective welfare. Reading that passage about a humble leader with socialized charisma, I wrote the name of a former boss next to the text.

Stay Away, but Be Accessible

As Shekshnia (2018) puts it, your role is the guide on the side. If you want center stage, look for another job.

> BM: *The CEO is the main face to the outside world; if you can't accept that fact, you have the wrong position.*

When asked for the Chair's biggest challenge, the most frequent answer was to leave the center stage to the CEO.

> BM: *The Chair must be able to withdraw and leave the CEO the operational role of the captain. If things are going badly, you take the blame; if things are going well, you pass on the credit or show little.*

As a Chair, you should give the CEO enough space to run the company, be present, and be accessible to her employees. If you are the sports team coach, you don't want the "owner" in the locker room—a principle accepted in the sports world that is not as evident in the business world.

As a former CEO, it may be a particular challenge for you as a Chair:

BM: As a former CEO, I have built up that company and know it so well; it is emotionally difficult to watch and keep myself out.

BM: It is a challenge and I have to tell myself that I—as a CEO—had not appreciated having a Chair who was doing my job.

It is natural to face those challenges if you care about the company and were involved more deeply in the past. Being aware of your needs, like being close to the action, enables you to manage yourself and your responses better. Don't forget that it is hard for the CEO to exclude you; be aware of how your needs may affect your behavior, what the CEO's needs are, and try not to put your needs before hers.

If the CEO is smart and trusts you, she will include you:

BM: Why don't you join me for the meeting? I need some help to sort this problem out.

A famous board saying goes: *keep the nose in but the fingers out*: stay away but be available and accessible. Unforeseen events will happen and small matters will need to be coordinated, especially before board meetings, the General Assembly, or the publication of results.

Staying away means giving the executive management space, but I believe that a Chair needs to spend time with the CEO, to understand their respective thinking and feeling about the role and the person, and to develop a trusted relationship. In line with many interviewees, I suggest that the Chair and CEO regularly block sufficient time for their one-to-one intense "routine interactions" (Roberts 2002). Since I also don't favor fixed boundaries between the two, it is natural that you need more discussion time. Many said they have a lonely job, so why not intensify the relationship between the Chair and the CEO?

Staying away but being accessible should not be perceived as meaning that the Chair is a bystander. The CEO and her team are well advised to treat you with respect; being available does not mean that people should contact you at will. The Chair should not feel that he can be called upon whenever management feels like it. Show the Chair that you also consider his needs, even when you don't need him. Let him know in advance—if possible—that you want to give him a call. And as a CEO, think about where you can explicitly invite the Chair to join a session.

Don't Be Shy About Being Clear: Manage Boundaries and, if Necessary, Say "No"

Most of the points mentioned so far lean toward a coaching attitude for the Chair. However, this should not be confused with a timid Chair who does not dare contradict the CEO. Then, the CEO controls the Chair. Shekshnia (2018) said that the board is the CEO's boss, not the Chair. If we follow that reasoning, we shift the power balance to the CEO because we weaken the Chair's function in an area where the entire board cannot compensate. The board is not close enough to the CEO, does not appreciate the subtle issues calling for a light intervention by the Chair. In setting boundaries and providing a counterbalance to the day-to-day business view of the CEO, the Chair has an important task that is impossible for the entire board to fulfill.

> BM: *The Chair and CEO both have to be strong; if the CEO is too strong, then the Chair has nothing to say; if the Chair is too strong, then CEO is the implementer. That's not possible either.*

The Chair has to have the courage and assertiveness to be clear if necessary, to dare to speak up vis-*à*-vis the CEO and say "no."

> BM: *The primary task of the Chair is to be the empathic companion of the CEO in the background; a big challenge for the Chair is to sense when to leave this primary role and to show rigid control and sharp boundaries. Both poles are needed; one rarely, but then, it is incredibly demanding.*

> BM: *The most hurtful thing the CEO can do to the Chair is move on with something of significance without discussing it with the Chair: I have seen such behavior. CEOs sometimes look for the edge of how far they can go; it is immature and unfortunate. You have to come down and address that issue quickly. These things typically don't happen by mistake; rather, it may be more the CEO's nature, and therefore you as a Chair and the board have to set clear boundaries.*

Boundary management is providing the framework. It is challenging, in particular, if it is not your natural tendency. Sharper boundaries are easier to handle and make it easier to keep somebody accountable. Still,

I favor the statement of Morais et al. (2018) that boundary management should be flexible and renegotiated occasionally. I am not a fan of clearly dedicated roles, such as the Chair is the brake and the CEO is the accelerator, although it is more role-appropriate than the CEO is pushier than the Chair. As Chair, you need to reflect on where to draw the line between free space and intervention.

Sometimes, if boundaries are crossed, you may say "no." Bregman (2013) offers nine practices to help you say "no"—for example, say no to the task, not the person, be appreciative, and be as resolute as your counterpart is pushy.

Setting boundaries and being clear is, however, not a common strength at the top. If you want an example of how friendly and gentle and often very unclear talks between bosses are, I can lead you to potential merger talks or a significant acquisition. A lot is at stake. In my experience, if the Chair or the CEO led those discussions, they came back with a very positive overall feeling. But it was often unclear what they seemingly agreed or discussed. While talks with third parties were worse, the same experience was often true in internal talks at the very top. Having been in charge of M&A for more than 20 years, I am undoubtedly biased, but my recommendation was often to leave the bosses out.

The M&A example refers in particular to talks between the Chairs or CEOs of companies considering a merger, a sensitive area clouded with personal wishes and fears. But it's not M&A alone; I observed many meetings between the Chair and the CEO where it was unclear what decisions were being made. The business world is full of "fast yes's" without knowing what we have committed to (Stanier 2016). If you prefer to have a comfortable meeting because you don't want to disappoint, you don't stress the obvious critical points. You are unclear because you want to be kind. But Brown (2018) puts it rightly: "Being unclear is unkind, being clear is kind." As Chair, being clear with your CEO does not imply that you know it all; rather, it helps avoid misunderstandings that can be costly and stress the relationship later on. "Being clear" can be applied to the content, the process, values issues, and boundaries.

BM: My dealing with emotions is quite developed. I am not easily hurt, but I can feel angry or irritated, and if that happens, I make it clear.

BM: I was just out with three board members, all three in big boards. We all see that the Chairs refuse to have private sessions, and they do so repeatedly. We have tried to find out the reasons, and we believe the Chairs don't dare to tell their CEOs that there are sessions where they can't be there.

In most areas, a Chair should not put his discretion above the CEO. But if the board of directors feels the need to reflect as a team, you should be assertive enough to do so.

If a manager delivers results but his or her behavior is not in line with fundamental values, you need to be clear.

BM: I was the CEO of a small business and we had to move offices, and I delegated the responsibility to my COO to get the new office prepared. And he was very organized as a project manager, but he was abrasive and hostile. He would yell at everyone. And I didn't deal with the behavioral issues. I alienated that entire company because I didn't step up and address that, you know, that sort of terrible behavior. I learned that the minute you lose your team's trust and respect, it takes forever to try and build it back. I tell that story all the time because in the future when I see behavior that I don't like, I will always pull that up, and I'll say I didn't deal with it the last time. I'm not going to make that mistake again. Sharing anecdotes and lessons learned contextualizes why "You cannot do this because..." and people listen.

If you know yourself well, you can assess how easy it is for you to be clear and set boundaries. Being aware of our natural inclination and knowing that the business world likes to be unclear, there is no harm in putting extra effort into being clear or, if you want to be unclear, then choosing to be so consciously.

Reflections on the Hypothetical Example

I will close with some reflections upon the fictional example at the beginning of this chapter.

The CEO informed the Chair early on, without knowing the complete picture, assessing what happened or what the next steps would be. With potentially bad news, I favor this type of disclosure. As Chair, you have a right to be informed early on of potential critical issues. But don't make it even harder for the CEO: appreciate being informed, stay calm, don't get angry.

The incident does not surprise the Chair because he has stressed that processes and compliance haven't had the necessary attention. Even if true, it is the wrong moment to address that and makes it less likely that the Chair will be informed early on in the future. There are reasons for the "bon mot" that good news travels fast and bad news doesn't travel at all.

This conflict also shows the tendency to heated debate when underlying values clash. While the CEO believes strongly in an empowering and learning culture, the Chair favors stability and reliability. Remembering the Riemann/Thomann cross, one axis was for our need for closeness and distance, the other for the duality of stability versus change. It fits the Chair's typical profile that he tends toward stability while the CEO pushes for change. The organization must reconcile stability, reliability, and exploitation with change, innovation, and exploration (Farjoun 2010). If the Chair and the CEO have different preferences, they must discuss them and may come to see the benefit. I had more than one CEO tell me during the interviews that the age gap with the Chair should not be too significant.

> BM: The truth is that Chairs should be younger. There is a tendency in Continental Europe to have somewhat old Chairs. And this is potentially a risk because of generation change, technological change, business change, and consumer change. Of course, on the other side, with an older Chair, there is experience, which is very important. But that has to be balanced a bit. Let me give you an example: discussing with the Chair how to move our clients to the cloud. That is a big decision. Who do I talk to? Of course, my technical people, of course, endless consultants. Then at the end of the day, I need to go and speak to the Chair. If the Chair is a brick-and-mortar kind of person, you feel a bit alone. Because I think he cannot help.

BM: The age gap between the Chair and the CEO shouldn't be too big. Your whole viewpoint on openness, communication, society, and technology, and many other things are so different that they can easily lead to inefficiencies.

The compliance issue in the hypothetical example confirms the Chair's view that management has too relaxed a leadership style, while the CEO is convinced that her route is the right one for the future. When others dismiss our values, we tend to react strongly (Edmondson 2012). Strong personal feelings, like the Chair's emotional attachment to the subsidiary, make such conflicts harder to resolve, which is why I suggest discussing your values in a neutral situation, not during a heated debate about a specific issue. Being aware that fundamental values are not the same is the first step; being further aware that opposing views correspond with your roles can help further. Understanding that neither wants to penalize the other but just has a different starting point helps build bridges. You might appreciate the other's view if it can help you both find a common middle ground for the company's benefit.

Instead of blaming, follow Stanier's guidance and ask the CEO any open questions about what is on her mind; what could be the next step? She is closer to the topic, has more information, more time to digest the news, and it is her job to handle it. Stay curious and listen to what thoughts she has. Say less, ask more. Show a coaching attitude, don't get into the driving seat.

The fact that the Chair mandated the audit department is a clear step in taking matters into his own hands. The CEO will think twice next time about informing him early on. The Chair could also have said, "Let's digest that news and sleep on it, and let's talk again tomorrow."

What about the CEO? Should she have disclosed her thoughts about selling the subsidiary? When attacked, if we have a fight rather than flight tendency, we tend to fight back. During my INSEAD studies, we heard Manfred Kets de Vries say many times to "hit when the iron is cold." The CEO in our example did not follow that advice. Maybe she was reacting instead of reflecting or, afraid that the Chair would hear preliminary thoughts of selling the subsidiary from elsewhere, decided on the spot to let him know before more harm could be done.

Going back to the Chair: assuming that the CEO did not know about the Chair's emotional connection to that subsidiary, what about sharing it? If he shares, he could influence the CEO so that the topic isn't raised again. However, it could be different if shared later, explaining why he reacted the way he did and state that he is open to selling the subsidiary if management is convinced it's the right move. This example clearly shows that sharing vulnerability depends on the context and intention. It is manipulative if you share it with the conscious intention that the CEO will give up the topic. If you share without reflecting, you don't know its effect because you haven't provided context. But if you communicate by explaining your reaction and even saying that you are open to the CEO's direction, it will help the relationship and future content discussions.

Finally, the Chair and CEO missed agreeing on the next steps. The CEO does not know when she should get back to him, and he did not share his thoughts about informing the entire board. In the end, it is his right to notify the board. However, it will affect his relationship with the CEO if he chooses to discuss issues like this with her or just act independently without having the benefit of her input. He could have said: *What are your thoughts about informing the board?* In the end, he could have said that he would like her to prepare a one-page briefing for the board, but that tomorrow they could discuss if the paper should be sent out immediately or if it would be more appropriate to wait.

> BM: *Sometimes, you have to protect the CEO even if you don't inform the board right away. That can be delicate, and I am not saying that the Chair should hide information from the board. But don't react hot-blooded and just share without reflection. Think about what to share, why to share, and when to share, and include the CEO in those thoughts. Just running to the board to cover yourself can be a disease of Chairs. If the board complains, later on, you should have the courage and character to tell the board that it was your decision. What you get in return from the CEO is trust.*

The quote above comes from a long-term Chair and shows how you, as a Chair, can apply some of the guiding principles in this chapter. Handling issues like this well can be a catalyst for a trusted relationship to be (further) developed or damaged.

CHAPTER 7

The Chair's Interaction With the Executive Board

The single biggest problem with communication is the illusion that it has taken place.

—George Bernard Shaw

Assumptions are the termites of relationships.

—Henry Winkler

Introduction

Interactions between the Chair and members of the executive board are a muddy area. The question is, how much direct communication between the Chair and the executive board should occur at all? Will the Chair have regular one-to-one with members of the executive board? What role has the Chair in helping executive board members learn and grow?

> *BM: A Chair should be more or less free to talk to anybody he likes, but in doing so, you have to respect the hierarchy and can't undermine or blindside the CEO.*

> *BM: I talk to all executive board members reasonably regularly for one thing or another; it is an open communication, not just with the CEO.*

> *BM: It depends on the company's size; in the smaller ones, almost as much as with the CEO; in the more prominent companies, it is more formalized and less frequent.*

However, many Chairs keep the communication to executive board members other than the CEO to a minimum. I stated earlier that cultural differences or the legal framework in my interviews did not play a significant role. An exception to this rule is the Chair's interaction with the executive board in Germany. There, the Chair often has few contact points, except to the CEO. One CEO even stated that his Chair has basically no contact with the "Vorstand" (executive board). It is not common for the Chair to have an office at the company's headquarters.

Apart from the German situation, the variety of answers regarding the Chair's interaction with the executive board was substantial. The Chair's interaction with management is an area where opinions broadly differ and an area that is dangerous ground for slip-ups. Therefore, I have provided some guiding principles to provide greater comfort (Figure 7.1).

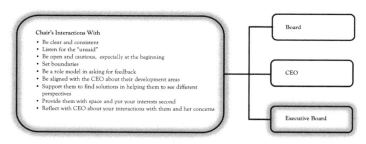

Figure 7.1 Chair's interaction with the executive board

Example

Let's assume an acquisition is on the horizon. As Chair, you have a regular meeting with the CFO. As the acquisition is an important issue, you discuss it. You are a reflective Chair who knows that you should be cautious in interfering with management's decision making, independent of whether the decision will have to be approved by the board of directors, so you mainly listen and ask questions. However, the CFO understands your listening as confirmation of his or her skeptical view regarding the acquisition. Two days later, you talk to the CEO, who is in favor of the acquisition. You act in the same way. The CEO leaves the meeting with the feeling that you will support the acquisition.

Does that sound familiar? Human beings generally prefer to have comfortable meetings and tend to hear what they choose to hear. So, as a Chair, you leaned slightly toward your respective dialogue partner during your conversation with first the CFO and later the CEO, and they heard what they wanted to hear. Even if, objectively speaking, you acted impartially, the perceived understanding can be quite different. With your exemplary listening attitude, you probably did not support the executive board to find consensus on the upcoming acquisition since both the CEO and the CFO left their respective meetings with an understanding that you share their view.

What conclusion can we draw from that example, and what else needs to be considered in the Chair's interaction with the executive board members?

To Do's

Be Clear and Consistent

Minor differences in what you say can be interpreted differently. Therefore, put extra effort into being clear and consistent. Even if you were just listening, it could have helped to communicate that you had not yet formed an opinion, preventing the implicit understanding and, finally, the misunderstanding. In general, it is probably wise to guard your opinion; otherwise, management will run to you early to influence you or delegate questions.

The role of a Chair is demanding. What you may indicate, or even what you don't say, is open to interpretation and speculation. It is easier to avoid specific topics like this example, which are on the table anyhow, being aware that such discussions can be harmful. However, it is tougher to avoid a gray area topic, like how member X of the executive board gets along with member Y. How is member Z interacting with a potential partner of your company? You will hear about the executive board from many different sources. Even if you do not hear explicit statements, you will get implicit messages and conclude from what is not said.

Listen for the "Unsaid"

The "unsaid" is especially important in an area where both dialogue partners know that they are in a muddy environment, tending to be even less transparent and outspoken.

As Chair, messages will be delivered to you during such talks. Therefore, we could argue that the Chair should have limited contact with the executive board. But we shouldn't be overly restrictive in those connections just in case things go wrong. To follow the restrictive approach, we would need more and more rules that miss the intended purpose, even if the intention was good. Restricted interactions could also apply to management, but today, the prevailing opinion is that interactions within management across hierarchical levels help the company.

For many years, I was responsible for politically sensitive fields like group human resource, group strategy and digital transformation, and M&A. My direct reports and others from my unit had direct access to the Group CEO. Were those meetings sometimes misused to send messages for their own purpose? Certainly! Was the open setup conducive to such messages? Absolutely! Did we face unpleasant situations because of this free setup? Yes! But should we have organized ourselves differently? No. Was it overall for the best of the company? Biased as I am, I would say "Yes."

In general, would I recommend an open approach? Now my lawyer soul appears, and I answer: it depends on how you deal with such situations. Can you talk about your concerns? Have you a trusted relationship? The better your relationship is, the more open and flexible your organization setup can be. Let it evolve. If necessary, you adapt and adjust.

Management interactions are different from interactions with the Chair. They happen more often, occur more in teams, and can be less contained. Therefore they have a less political cloud. All reasons why we shouldn't directly apply arguments valid for open management interactions to interactions with the Chair. That said, the Chair and executive team's interactions can have many advantages, so we shouldn't "throw the baby out with the bathwater." I favor an open but cautious approach.

Be Open but Cautious, Especially at the Beginning

Being cautious seems to be right, especially in the beginning, when you are less familiar with the executive board members because either you or they are new in the job. Once you start to talk about delicate issues, it will be hard to stop in the future. You will likely believe that it shows how well your relationship has developed, but it can make it harder to be disciplined and rein in your curiosity. Favoring a cautious approach may be considered out of line with the overall open attitude expressed in the section about trust and showing vulnerability, but it is less risky to become more accessible with time.

Set Boundaries

Brown (2018) pointed out very clearly that we also have to observe boundaries. Sharing has to have an intention and should be done with reflection. So sometimes, you may ask an executive board member why they are telling you something. Setting boundaries will have an immediate effect, and a member will think twice about whether they should share such an issue next time. You may have to sacrifice your curiosity, doing so for the benefit of a hygienic climate and a well-functioning executive board and, ultimately, the company.

Be a Role Model in Asking for Feedback

Boundaries also play an important role in asking for feedback. I would encourage you to ask for feedback from the executive board (see also Chapter 11 for board review input). You can be the role model for a learning attitude toward the whole company but be aware you could get feedback meant to influence your views of content rather than behaviors, mainly if directed to specific content already on the horizon or on the executive board members' horizon. Be aware of the feedback you receive; it could serve self-centered motives.

But, if you are open to honest feedback, it will help management be more accessible for general feedback, particularly from you. You can have a significant influence on them.

Be Aligned With the CEO About Their Development Areas

If you and the CEO are aligned on the executive board members' development areas, you can be a potent team in developing your top management team. In my opinion, the Chair can play a particular role as head of talent management. But if the feedback of the Chair and CEO toward the executive board pulls in opposite directions, you create anxiety and paralysis, meaning no development will occur. Getting mixed messages increases our natural habit of not changing behavior, so explicit alignment is crucial. If the CEO realizes that you can help her, she may develop a different attitude to your talks with executive board members.

BM: I talk every quarter with the CEO about each executive board member's performance and development issues. Only when aligned and agreed upon will I address issues directly with an executive board member.

Support Them to Find Solutions in Helping Them View Different Perspectives

Referring to the acquisition example again, instead of implying that you share their respective views, you could help each executive board member better understand the opposing view, increasing the likelihood that the team will find their own solutions by demonstrating an empowering attitude.

BM: I act a little bit like a coach to all members of the executive board team to help them see the perspective of others. As you get older and have more experience and distance, you learn that one shouldn't be too dismissive of other people's viewpoints, so you can help managers to see the other's perspective.

Provide Them With Space and Put Your Interests Second

Favoring an open approach between the Chair and the executive board should not be confused with the Chair sitting on the executive board. You may like the action and therefore want to be close to it. As much as that's understandable, it's probably not what the team needs to flourish. Having a Chair that is too close makes it hard for the CEO to form a team; therefore, you also should not sit physically close to the executive board.

Be very selective in joining executive board meetings. A good rule is that you only attend by invitation of the CEO for a particular topic.

Don't give the executive board members the right to veto. *A CEO complained that the Chair said to the executive board team that they should not bother him as long as they don't share the same view on that issue.* How should the CEO lead under these circumstances? An unusual situation may justify such behavior; in general, it is a no-go.

Reflect With the CEO About Your Interactions With Them and Her Concerns

It is likely that the CEO has angst over your interactions with the executive board but has trouble addressing it, and you have not raised it with her.

Asking Chairs how their CEOs feel about their talks with the executive board members, it was not uncommon to get a response such as:

> BM: I have never felt in any case that the CEO feels my talks are undermining her authority in any way. Everybody seems to be happy with those open talks. But your question motivates me to ask her explicitly how she feels about it and not just me presuming that it is okay for her.

Don't take those interactions for granted: clarify concerns and address opportunities. The CEO is in a vulnerable situation. Therefore, you need to be sensitive, ask about her concerns, and listen to those she may not explicitly address. Does she feel comfortable? What are her boundaries? What did you learn? Where do you need more alignment? Don't swat away concerns from the CEO lightheartedly. As Chair, you need to listen well to the "unsaid." I would strongly recommend that the Chair and CEO have honest talks about those interactions and their pitfalls.

CHAPTER 8

Interactions Between the Board of Directors and the Executive Board

You can make more friends in two months by becoming interested in other people than you can in two years by trying to get other people interested in you.

—Dale Carnegie

The greatest compliment that was ever paid me was when someone asked me what I thought and attended to my answer.

—Henry David Thoreau

The Board of Directors and the Executive Board: A Problematic Relationship?

The relationship between the board of directors and the executive board is generally not particularly intense. Other than in Germany (due to the restricted role of the board), a Chair's standard view was:

BM: My simple answer is: not enough. Most of the board interaction with management tends to be with the CEO and the CFO; very little exposure to the rest of the management team, which is not great.

Many boards favor more interactions than they currently have:

BM: We make an effort to create more interactions by including a range of agenda items so that different executive members can come and present; or just meet and greet, cocktails before board meetings or after, just so that there's broader exposure and at least names and faces become more familiar to the board members.

BM: I think it's healthy for the board to have broad exposure; that's the only way you can get a profound perspective of how the business is doing.

However, critical voices were prominent as well:

BM: In reality, board members love to bypass the CEO and (mis-)use their committee function to do it.

Committee work offers excellent opportunities for the board and the management to interact on shared tasks (see Chapter 5). But the interactions between the board members and the executive board members also have the potential to cloud the Chair and CEO relationship.

BM: I have made various observations, and [it is] also partly bitter experiences. It is a mutual weighing up of the relationship between the board of directors and the executive board. What should not happen is a life of its own between single board members and executive board members who bypass the Chair. This leads to bad culture: suddenly, conspiratorial activities and often questions about people arise (did you see? is this the right one? what did he do? etc.). It needs a particular discipline and order for such contacts to be handled. And it should be informed about the content of the conversation—no secrets allowed.

Let's take, for example, the head of the audit-and-risk committee and the CFO. It's good if they get along, but that can also run the risk of creating an "unholy alliance." Assume that the CFO, to build a trusted relationship with the head of that committee, shares more than intended about how the figures or dividends might look in the future. What may be suitable for this particular relationship may be bad for the relationship with the Chair or the CEO. Both may lose control over important issues if the head of the audit-and-risk committee and the CFO become too close. What makes it worse is that this relationship often exists in a closed bubble; sensitive information shared or impressions made are not quickly corrected. In order to mitigate undesirably close bonds between board members and executive board members (another connection would be head of the compensation committee and head of HR), I favor the Chair providing ample space for informal talks between the board and management in general, consistent with earlier comments, to create psychological safety (see Chapter 2). For different reasons, I recommend that the head of the audit-and-risk committee talk to other relevant managers—such as the head of accounting. It reduces the danger of those one-to-one connections.

Sharing in one-to-ones is particularly tricky. But even if the CFO shares relevant information in the audit committee meeting, it should be obvious to those attending that he or she is aligned with the CEO and that this information was intended to be shared. If not, unnecessary trust issues can appear between the CEO and the board.

The overall relationship between the board and the executive board has to be seen in a broader context than just who shares what and with whom.

> *BM: I often observed a kind of cynicism in the management. Oh, those board members don't understand the business and want to know things that are not relevant and cause us more work that doesn't add any value.*

> *BM: Executive board members should like sitting with the board, which is rarely the case; the Chair has won when the CEO is looking forward to the next board meeting.*

Those two quotes pointedly describe how management often thinks about the board, very much in line with my personal experience. Being secretary of the board of directors for over 10 years, I learned early on about the needs of the board of directors and the critical attitude of management toward the board. Since I also had a management function at that time, mainly as a general counsel, I tried to build a bridge between the board and the management. A former boss even told me once that I was "half board member," because I tried to help management see the board's perspective.

Later in my career, when I was on boards myself, and especially in the audit committee in a different industry, I experienced the considerations of board members even more. Should I ask that particular question? Should I demand that overview, causing management to do more work, to understand a specific issue better?

Coming back to the two aforementioned quotes: Do members of the board of directors perceive management's underlying critical feeling? It is not uncommon for board members to have self-doubts about their impact (remember that quote in the introduction about "the doghouse being for the dog and the supervisory board being for the cat"). It is not easy for a board member sandwiched between the Chair and the executive board to add value with the limited time available. When in doubt, humans look for signals to confirm their assumptions. Small signals from management can be disastrous in enforcing self-doubt or shame-like feelings. Negative feelings are more potent the more you care about your role and try to add value. To add to that problematic picture, boards are often well paid, adding the self-doubts of being worth the money. To quote Brown (2018): "The fear of being irrelevant is a huge shame trigger that we are not addressing at work."

You may think that I'm overstating the case. And maybe it is only a slight sense of shame, but it is unpleasant to question ourselves whether we add value. It is more profound than a feeling of guilt because we have not done something wrong, for which we could apologize. We shy away from talking about such feelings because it is too unpleasant. This is mainly a topic for the Chair to address with his board; if we do not talk about those feelings, they will have a more significant impact on us and more control over our life (see Chapter 2—what team members need to flourish). Therefore, it is helpful if the board and the management team can reflect upon their tasks and feelings in an appropriate setting (see Part III about board reflection and board review).

If the board members feel less than confident about their impact, they are probably unconsciously more critical of the executive board, making the executive board feel underappreciated, and more critical with the board of directors—a classic vicious cycle.

With much time spent preparing for the board of directors' meeting, the executive board may feel underappreciated and wasted time on the wrong issues. Ideally, it would prefer to spend its time leading the company, developing employees, talking to customers, and reflecting on strategy. The Chair and the board are important but should not take too much time from operations. Ideally, the board and the Chair support the CEO and her team; often, however, the CEO uses up resources to manage the Chair and the board of directors. The executive board should take the board of directors very seriously and treat them respectfully, but its focus should be on improving the company rather than satisfying the board.

Interactions between board members and executive board members should support their relationship. I favor executive board members participating in the board meeting to understand better how the board ticks. Committees are an excellent opportunity to confirm the self-worth of board members and consolidate interactions with the executive board members. I have been participating in audit committees for more than 20 years and was the link between the compensation committee and management for a similar length of time. Those two committees offer significant interactions and potential between board and executive board members without the Chair or the CEO always being present. However, everyone involved needs to show discipline in his or her interactions.

What can the players do to sustain a good working relationship between the board and the executive management? What guiding principles can help the executive board members and board of directors so that fewer negative feelings arise from their interactions, and they both benefit?

Some points appear on both sides of the equation. Since they have a different emphasis, I will describe them separately.

To Do's—Board of Directors to Executive Board

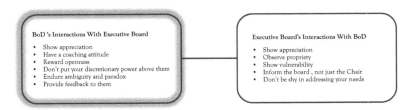

Figure 8.1 Board of directors' interaction with executive board

Show Appreciation

The board of directors plays a decisive role in supporting, motivating, encouraging, and challenging the executive board.

> BM: Everyone on the executive board, who has a much more substantial impact on the company's everyday life, and has to meet the pressure and demands of all stakeholder groups, is much more effective knowing that they have the support of the board of directors. Anything else is no fun; I wouldn't want to work on an executive board with constant arguments with the board of directors.

> BM: After a board session, the executive board members should not leave feeling the need to recover; that can't be. The board of directors should not be stingy with recognition and appreciation while still being critical.

The quotes speak for themselves. Showing appreciation is critical and serves as a grease for the board–management relationship.

Have a Coaching Attitude

Not showing a coaching attitude, but rather telling the management what to do, often has its roots in not reflecting about your role or having a strong desire to prove your worth by making statements. "Making statements" behavior can be observed in both board and management meetings. "Saying less and asking is more" is as valid here as for the relationship between the Chair and the CEO.

> BM: There are board members who know a bit of everything; often, former CEOs do not differentiate between their roles. Asking open-ended questions shows an attitude of being interested in another person's thoughts. You can always be critical later on and disagree but start by being curious.

> BM: You can challenge management, offer a piece of advice, but you have to be careful not to do its job.

A company's board of directors is often passive; it receives what the management has discussed intensively in advance, with which the

Chair has already (to a certain extent) agreed. So, if something goes awry, one of them may finally see the chance to contribute actively. This reflex is as natural as it is dangerous because it can lead to a hyperactive board at the wrong moment. It can also lead to bad news not traveling to the board of directors or only arriving when everything has already been decided. The distribution of tasks between the board of directors and management favors this reflex-like action. For this very reason, and not for some Machiavellian intent, the board of directors should also have its areas of activity where the board is in the arena, such as talks with major investors about governance issues and culture. Being in the arena makes a difference, but if that's where you always want to be, then the board of directors of larger companies is not the place to find contentment.

Reward Openness

For trust between the board of directors and management, management must be open to insecurities (showing vulnerability) and potentially bad news. The board of directors should appreciate this openness and not reflexively fall into activity mode.

> BM: *The openness in the relationship between the board and the management requires that management also reports about its failures and imminent risks and enthusiastically about its successes. The openness between the two bodies requires that the board of directors does not always know everything better. Openness has to be earned by giving from a currency that is precious to you; for the board, the currency is the authority; for management, the currency is being successful and therefore also shares where it was not successful.*

Real Example

Different internal finance teams evaluated the external auditor, and the auditor assessed the finance teams. We thought that was helpful for their respective working relationship. I wanted to share this information with the audit committee, but some felt that it was a bad idea because the purpose of the evaluation was to improve their working relationship. I agreed with that but stressed that we should share the information because the external auditor is the most critical partner for the audit committee. I told the executive board that I would suggest the audit committee not to take ownership and introduce actions. Not surprisingly, the audit committee did try to own the topic but eventually agreed that the external auditor and the finance units should try to improve specific issues first, and the audit committee would get a status update later.

Honor openness and don't try to own topics; otherwise, you create a disincentive to share.

Boards often criticize a zero-risk attitude in management. Still, taking ownership of a problematic issue incentivizes risk avoidance and bad news not traveling.

Don't Put Your Discretionary Power Above Them

Having the power and using it are two different coins of a medal:

BM: Just because you are the highest authority should not mean that the board of directors has to decide everything.

BM: In the last board meeting, we decided to invest in a factory for a new product class we worked on for many years. I said "yes," but I would have been surprised if it worked. But why should I know it better? Management invested a lot in it and knew what it was talking about. I could only answer instinctively. I should challenge and ask questions, but I have to be cautious not to put my gut feeling above management's view.

Boards of directors have a lot of power, but they are well advised to use it only if needed. Since management runs the business, it is usually not advisable for the board of directors to simply overrule them. It can frustrate management, lead to an attitude of being less generous in what it shares, or result in the opposite of delegating decisions to the board of directors. The board of directors should challenge management but ultimately support it; don't put your discretional judgment above management when in doubt.

Endure Ambiguity and Paradox

I will start with a quote from Cannon (1996) that reflects the current business reality better than ever: "Many paradoxes are caused by the hangover of one set of assumptions or beliefs into a new age or environment and proliferate when change is dramatic or rapid. Paradoxes emerge when beliefs or assumptions fail to keep up with external change."

As a member of an executive board, I was responsible for strategy. We were facing a challenging environment where it was daring to claim to know the right direction for the future. The tension between the core business and the "bets team" grew; these innovation teams were named "bets team" because of their role in "placing bets" on the future.

Lewis (2000) calls this tension "the learning paradox" between the old and the new, between the comfort of the past and the uncertainty of the future. One of the questions for the CEO was: What shall we lay out on the board table? One would assume the key strategic questions since that is the board's responsibility. But as Fredberg (2014) wrote, "CEOs are the messengers of the solution and not the problems." The board expects the management to bring clearly held views to the board. Showing vulnerability, and thereby getting complexity, and "ambidextrous" issues (as in, ones to which you can see both sides) to the board can produce anxiety and often defensive responses (Lewis 2000). Consciously accepting ambiguity and paradoxes is vital for the board (Morais et al. 2018). As a Chair put it:

> BM: Sometimes, we cannot stand the anxiety of having a problem without a solution, so we'd rather take a gun and shoot in order to immediately release the anxiety, only to understand later that we have not made progress.

Such an attitude calls again for self-awareness and reflection; otherwise, you may react defensively. Being aware of the source of discomfort allows you to sit in pain more easily. Howard Book described this in an INSEAD lecture as *capable of containing and tolerating ambiguity and paradox*; not rushing to closure, resisting shooting the messenger, and showing the vulnerability and openness to discuss critical issues with the board.

An easy but unsatisfactory escape from uncomfortable feelings is to trust the experts, thereby unconsciously divesting responsibility for a particular decision and allaying individual fears of not having enough knowledge. The more persuasive the individual, the higher in the hierarchy, the more likely the board will follow him or her without challenge. This risk is much higher if you have a Chair who is a second expert after the CEO. Under these circumstances, the board is likely to feel comfortable letting those two determine the course and manage the tension (see research by Morais et al. 2018).

However, this easy way out is not consistent with the core function of the board: dealing with the company's strategic challenges.

The board must be aware of ambiguity and paradoxes; the more complex and dynamic organizations become, the more traditional "either/or" thinking oversimplifies management practices and demands. As Lewis (2000) states, "Managing paradoxical tensions denotes not compromise between flexibility and control, but awareness of their simultaneity." To have fruitful discussions about strategy, an attitude of accepting ambiguity and paradoxes is essential in order to have a management team come forward with the issues that matter. It is the mirror behavior a board has to show if it wants a CEO willing to show vulnerability.

Provide Feedback to Them

The board's central task is to provide feedback. Reflection and feedback for the executive board are rare.

> *BM: On different boards, we do a 360° with the executive board. It runs reasonably well. Surprisingly, it operates best in China, where the whole board of directors will conduct interviews with every executive team member and spend two days doing it. And the intent is not for people to love one another. The objective is to get feedback, assess*

alignment, to flesh out relationship issues between team members. It's a great exercise. It's a significant investment in time, but it's well worth the time and money. And, very importantly, you also begin to reconcile why certain things aren't working as well as they should be.

This quote certainly does not represent the norm but shows a board investing time in the development of the executive board. I have not included the feedback point for the "to do's" of the executive board because it is difficult without being specifically asked. However, I strongly favor the idea that the executive board can provide feedback to the entire board (see Chapter 11 about board review).

To Do's—Executive Board to Boards of Directors

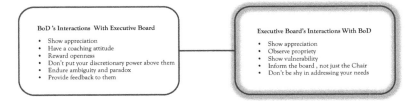

BoD's Interactions With Executive Board

- Show appreciation
- Have a coaching attitude
- Reward openness
- Don't put your discretionary power above them
- Endure ambiguity and paradox
- Provide feedback to them

Executive Board's Interactions With BoD

- Show appreciation
- Observe propriety
- Show vulnerability
- Inform the board, not just the Chair
- Don't be shy in addressing your needs

Figure 8.2 Executive board's interaction with board of directors

Show Appreciation

Bearing in mind the role of the board of directors, the executive board must have a humble and appreciative attitude toward it. Try to understand its needs; see its perspective; be socially aware of what you should be as a leader. An excellent way to show appreciation is in the way you prepare for board meetings. Documents don't need to be perfect, but they should allow the directors to understand and assess the key issues. They should be concise and show the essential pros and cons of a particular topic. Sit back and take the time to consider what the board already knows, where you should start, what the key message will be, and how you will present it.

Being aware that the board could have self-doubts should help the management put extra effort into preparing well. This does not mean that you have to produce more pages—quite the opposite. But it is a task that you can't delegate because you have to have experience in interacting with the board to know where to meet them. This is another reason I believe that executive board members should participate in full at board meetings. Encourage board members to ask questions, don't assume too much knowledge on very specific subjects. It is important how you react to questions if you want them to ask questions in the future. The way you express appreciation is less explicit but no less important.

Observe Propriety

One-to-ones, especially, offer many opportunities to cross the line; if a board member asks you questions in a friendly, informal way, you may feel flattered or obliged to answer. You may want to take the opportunity to show how much knowledge you have in areas that may not be the core of your responsibility; as a result, you could end up engaging in a conversation that is far outside your territory.

I am not advocating that you behave overly cautiously. I generally favor openness, but one-to-ones can be the wrong place for that attitude since they invite sharing and being open. Therefore, be aware of what you share, be clear and consistent, and observe propriety in how you behave.

Show Vulnerability

While one-to-ones can be dangerous for the reasons described above, a meeting of the entire board is an area where openness is much less hazardous. Board members will tend to reciprocate openness if you demonstrate it. Building trust is a two-way path.

In my experience, presentations to the board of directors are often too sanitized and abstract. They don't focus on where an executive team had, or still has, doubts. Lacking the everyday familiarity of those running the business, it can be hard for board members to grasp certain topics. You may have little serious discussion, or discussion for the sake of it, rather than about the critical issues. It can even be a deliberate tactic to lead the board to discuss something less essential, thereby avoiding something crucial. If members of the executive team act such that you are showing vulnerability in showing insecurity, the board of directors needs to be prepared and allow a feeling of ambiguity (see earlier in this chapter).

The more critical and future-oriented a topic is, the more showing vulnerability has value; be choiceful with such a philosophy and use it on most relevant issues. Otherwise, you will need more time for board meetings, making neither board members nor your team happier. Showing vulnerability should also not be confused with delegating decisions to the board, but rather in being transparent where you, as a team or individual, have struggled.

Inform the Board, Not Just the Chair

Shekshnia (2018) wrote that the board is the CEO's boss, not the Chair alone. Whether we follow that view or not, the CEO must manage the relationship with the Chair and the entire board of directors. One crucial point in building trust with the board is how you deal with potentially bad news. Some topics can remain for the moment with the Chair, but, as CEO, you should be intentional in informing the board early on; the CEO is responsible to the board and not just to the Chair. It is easier for the Chair to decide to hold back certain information than for the CEO. Informing early on is crucial for a trusted relationship, and in informing early on, "be open and realistic."

Don't Be Shy in Addressing Your Needs

The previous points were in favor of the board, but the last takes a different direction. Trying to have a good relationship with the board does not mean that you should not be firm if the board tries to interfere with you leading the company.

If the board wants you to prepare documentation about something, by all means, try to see its perspective and ask questions. But if you are convinced that fulfilling that task adds no value, don't be shy in addressing it. The more aligned you are as an executive team, the easier it is to handle those issues.

PART III

Reflection and Board Evaluation

CHAPTER 9

Benefits From Different Forms of Reflection

Leadership and learning are indispensable to each other.
—John F. Kennedy

Without reflection, we go blindly on our way, creating more unintended consequences, and failing to achieve anything useful.
—Margaret J. Wheatley

Part III describes the benefits of reflection for boards and the different forms it can take. The trend for boards to put greater focus on their dynamics will make board workshops and board evaluation more popular: in several jurisdictions, the law requires board evaluations. I hope that those board evaluations will not foster a tick-box mentality, focusing on regulatory and governance issues, but will look at the inner dynamics of boardrooms, where I see the most significant potential.

If we combine reflecting and learning, we are on the path of reaping our potential and individual growth—morally, personally, psychologically, emotionally, and cognitively. I have often referred to the benefits of a reflective personality and reflection sessions. A reflective mindset is related to self-awareness and the awareness of others, a crucial pillar for any successful leader (see Chapter 3).

For many years, I was a feedback fan. I still am. However, today, I'm an even bigger fan of reflection, especially in a group that fulfills its task as a part-time job, like the board of directors. Feedback tends to promote technical proficiency, can put you into a pigeonhole projected by others, and can be pointed or hurtful. Many psychological theories exist as to why people are so sensitive to hearing about their imperfections. The threat of critical feedback often leads us to practice maladaptive behaviors (procrastination, denial, jealousy, self-sabotage), which can harm our health and environment (Jackman and Strober 2003).

Feedback is undoubtedly a vital input factor. But without reflection, we will not accept and make use of critical feedback. Since our public image is so important to us, individual feedback in a group setting demands a mature team. Joint reflection is not easy but, in my opinion, very promising for a group setting.

When we reflect, we usually look back on past actions. As Peter Drucker said: "Follow effective action with quiet reflection. From the quiet reflection, will come even more effective action." Quiet reflection means *self-reflection*—looking into the mirror and describing what we see, a way of assessing ourselves. If our social mirror is mainly made up of the opinions and projections of people around us, it is like a "reflection in the crazy mirror room at the carnival" (Covey 2020). How others perceive us is vital to discover our blind spots but first of all, we should take responsibility for our development by reflecting upon ourselves. We should avoid sitting only on the receiving side of feedback. We are in control. We should own responsibility for our development, starting with self-awareness and self-reflection. If I compare my former employer's in-house training offerings, we went from teaching mainly know-how to personal development, where reflection practices play a central role. According to a global report from Egon Zehnder (2018), half of the interviewed CEOs acknowledged that they require personal reflection and would benefit from it. If we reflect with a board buddy about board meetings, which can help our learning and build relationships, we should be disciplined enough not to bad-mouth other board members; the focus should be on what *we*, as individuals, can do better.

Schön (2017), in his famous book *The Reflective Practitioner,* introduced the concept of "reflection-in-action," where you act and reflect at the same time. Take a negotiation or heated debate where you have to decide whether to speak or stay silent in an instant. Let's assume that you have agreed with your team, not to mention a competing offer at that stage. But then, something you hear in the negotiation makes it questionable whether to stick to that course of action. You may talk and at the same time observe and reflect upon what you have heard or not heard and adjust your approach accordingly. Reflection-in-action can help you choose an appropriate response to any form of stimulus (Covey 2020).

Schön (2017) argues that managers may reflect in action but seldom reflect upon that reflection-in-action, and even less make that reflection accessible to others. So, later on, you may share with your team why you chose to mention the competing offer at that stage. Maybe your team had similar thoughts, or perhaps they would have chosen a different way forward. Jointly reflecting helps develop a better understanding of the situation, the parties involved, and yourself.

Reflection-in-action can be conscious or intuitive. If we don't reflect, we have trouble articulating our thoughts. Maybe we are not understood by others and, since we don't let others participate in our reflection, little learning occurs. Perhaps our reflective thoughts could benefit from contributions by others, or others could benefit from our reflective thinking. Suppose you openly address your reflection and lead the team at that moment with your reflective intervention to a meta-level. In that case, this public reflection-in-action can be of outstanding value. Reflection-in-action can smooth a heated debate and lead a team back to the path of virtue (see Chapter 2). Edmondson (2012) stresses the importance of reflection for an effective team, favoring a reflective mindset/reflection-in-action over formal reflection sessions.

However, the formal setting of board meetings may favor a dedicated reflection session. This does not preclude each member from having a reflective mind that is "on" at all times. If you observed something significant, you should take note. A great team may have the strength and cohesiveness that an immediate reflection-in-action is accepted or even welcome. The Chair has indeed more acceptance to act in such a way. The ability to halt and ask where the team is right now can be compelling, but it is also a complex intervention, at least if you have an ongoing heated debate.

For any leader, to have the ability to "reflect in action" is a tremendous capability. However, my focus is on *reflection after the action* and reflecting as a team. I call it "joint reflection after the action" in the board context, at the end of the board meeting when the decision has been made, and agenda points discussed. Then when we have reflected on our own, we can share our reflections. However, joint reflection is not just sharing what you remembered; if you listen and reflect on what you hear, you reflect together. Joint reflection allows us to develop points together, enabling us to form and communicate issues in our heads that we could not entirely express on our own. Or maybe, you had a thought, you didn't dare mention it, but a peer's statement encouraged you to make your reflection public as well.

Reflection requires leaders to do several things they are typically not keen on: adopt a mindset of not knowing, tolerate an attitude of inefficiency, take personal responsibility, and show vulnerability. As managers, we are action biased. Reflection needs an attitude of accepting silence and the capacity to sustain reflective inaction. The process often increases psychological safety and leads to group cohesiveness, valuable insights, and even breakthroughs. It can also lead to feelings of discomfort, defensiveness, and irritation (Porter 2017). As a general rule, more profound progress is not possible without uncomfortable feelings, especially if we touch upon and thereby challenge our behavior. As Erik van de Loo liked to say at INSEAD: "Every change comes with a loss." Being aware of that helps us endure discomfort when reflecting and then improving by adapting our behavior as a team. Reflection serves a purpose. We want to learn and strengthen our board interactions, how we function as a team, and our efficiency. Learning and reflection need each other. What could fit better than one of my favorite quotes from Confucius: "Learning without reflection is a waste, reflection without learning is dangerous."

Reflection and learning demand a mindset where we say "yes" to uncertainty and tension. The tendency to avoid ambiguity, suspense, and stress is natural and human but required for deeper learning (Bogusz 2013). An organization or a body like the board will—without reflection—tend to stay on its course (Kayes 2017). A board is prone to stay its course, signifying that it has not enough reflection time. Boards certainly do not get much feedback, so talking about the board itself may not be easy.

Reflection sessions after the board meeting can find essential issues to reflect upon more broadly. Above all, they should increase the feeling of belonging to a team, gain psychological safety, and increase readiness to participate.

BM: We introduced a joint reflection session for the last 30 minutes; we try to sit back and avoid that action mode we are always in. The reflection sessions have created a more psychologically safe and open environment for the team; we share where we are doing well or struggling and ask for help.

Minor irritations, concerns, and insecurities can be addressed; these issues often lose significance when the board clears the air. You may hear small observations which allow you to fine-tune your behavior at the next meeting or be encouraged in a specific behavior. Leaving the board meeting with positive feelings is vital for a strong team.

As my INSEAD thesis (Sieber 2019a) demonstrated, reflection sessions are essential for boards. Joint reflection sessions within the board were the main trigger for psychological safety, voice, and open dialogue. Reflective practices are becoming more common in the corporate world. I strongly recommend that a board has *short reflection sessions* after each board meeting. I also favor that each board has, once a year, a two-day board retreat or, as I call it, as a reflection advocate, *reflection workshop*—which I will discuss in Chapter 11.

CHAPTER 10

Joint Reflection

When, How, and About What?

Sometimes, you have to look back in order to understand the things that lie ahead.

—Yvonne Woon

Nothing ages people like not thinking.

—Christopher Morley

When?

"Reflection after the action" implies a session at the very end of a board meeting. Some suggest it before the last agenda points so that the reflection session is less likely to be a victim of time. I prefer to have it at the end because it calls for a change in mindset; therefore, I suggest having a short break before the reflection session starts. Since the executive board should not be present, there are also practical reasons to do it at the very end: the executive board members can go for a drink (more likely work on the accrued e-mails) instead of waiting outside. If you make a clear break, you also provide room for executive board members to say goodbye instead of just walking out of the room. This gives a different tone and can be the opportunity to have a swift word with a board member about something that occurred earlier in the meeting. My last employer's board of directors introduced reflection sessions due to my INSEAD thesis, but we had to leave the room without a break. I missed the goodbye as well as the chance to get some things out of the way. That said, the end is the right place for the reflection session. As a Chair, make clear that this agenda item will not be sacrificed. I know from personal experience that this is a real challenge.

How?

Figure 10.1 lists some points to consider.

Reflection Session After the Action

- Take a short break, then let anybody reflect for 5 minutes on their own
- Agree on the purpose of the reflection session
- Structure it lightly
- Stay open, be flexible but don't lose focus
- Take note of bigger points to be addressed later
- No need to have long session–be short and pragmatic
- Just do it: don't judge yourself and others, and learn on your way

Figure 10.1 Reflection session after the action

Take a Short Break, Then Let Everybody Reflect for Five Minutes on Their Own

To get into a reflective mindset as a group, we first need to set time apart. We probably need a short break to get some fresh air. I would give everyone five minutes to sit quietly; preferably, you took notes with your reflective attitude during the meeting. Nevertheless, reflecting on your own is essential and will help the session's quality. But show self-discipline and set an example because this is neither an additional break nor the time to work on your e-mails.

Agree on the Purpose of the Reflection Sessions

Reflection sessions at the end of each board meeting are about yourselves, no one else, particularly not management. They serve to make the board team better and improve your interactions both as a team and with management. I purposefully don't use the word "efficient" because it leans too much toward having fast and smooth meetings. Instead, a good outcome is for reflection sessions to help the board feel safer—so you are more likely to address critical issues—or to allow you to discuss strategic matters next time in a more meaningful way.

Structure It Lightly

Structuring a reflection session after-action makes it more focused and lowers the mental barrier toward mentioning something. A tried and tested structure distinguishes between outcome, process, and relationship to which I will return shortly.

You can then go around the room, starting with someone who is not the Chair, with each person going through each of their points. Or you can leave it open so that anyone who wants to can add something to what has already been said. It is excellent if all members participate, but I wouldn't force the issue. If nothing important emerges, it is, after all, valuable to remain silent and listen. A comment by a peer may also trigger a reflection point you want to share.

Stay Open, Be Flexible but Don't Lose Focus

Sometimes, a reflection that seems far from serving its intended purpose may trigger a breakthrough. Stay open, listen carefully, and be flexible. However, don't fall into the tempting trap of talking about anything other than about you as the board. As Chair, you need awareness and subtlety to stir those reflection sessions, and the quality of moderator comes into play. Try to control your impulse to intervene early on. Don't discourage members from reflecting; however, if the team loses focus, it is your job to steer the discussion back to the sessions' purpose.

Take Note of Bigger Points To Be Addressed Later

A point related to focusing on ourselves as the topic of discussion is if a board member offers a reflective thought about a big issue—like the company's purpose. As Chair, I would not intervene even if such a topic should not be the primary purpose of the reflection session after the action. We should not feel a need to react to any reflection. Let it flow. If you intervene early, the perception can be that you don't want to discuss that topic. If another board member follows up, this can show a need for the board to talk about it. Then, it might be the time to intervene: not in "fobbing off" whoever raised the topic, but by postponing the discussion of something so significant to a dedicated session, encouraging everybody to give this point reflection time later. You may add that you are happy to receive thoughts about how and when to tackle the issue. This way, you bring the board back to the session's real objective without prematurely deciding if there is a need to discuss the company's purpose. However, raising big picture questions can also be a defensive move by a board member who does not want to talk about his or her behavior—and we are back to the real objective of the reflection session and the previous point about focus.

No Need to Have Long Session—Be Short and Pragmatic

Reflection sessions are not like chocolate, with the majority of people being fans. I know reflection addicts and haters—at least in a group context. For the addicts, the longer it lasts, the better, especially in a group setting. It nourishes the need for belonging. But there is usually no need for an extended reflection session after the action; these sessions should be pragmatic and short. As a rule, half an hour for a board is sufficient. In a critical situation where the team needs more time, you will end up with an extended session, but that should be the exception.

Just Do It: Don't Judge Yourself and Others, and Learn on Your Way

Try to develop a nonjudgmental attitude: don't be overly critical about individual input, yours or anybody else's. The process will feel more comfortable and relaxed. The skill of a good reflection session needs to be learned. It doesn't necessarily come easily to begin with. Why should we be perfect if we haven't had much experience, especially in a board setting?

Accept that some people will be relatively quiet.

BM: As the one who leads the reflection session, the biggest challenge for me is that not everybody opens up; how do I prove it feels safe to speak? How can I engage all? How do I manage the different needs

and dynamics for people to open up? But I have to tell myself that
we just started the journey. Sometimes, I call out some of my team
members when I believe their contribution can be valuable. Later, I
often receive encouraging remarks from people who were silent in the
reflection session.

As a Chair or CEO, it is normal that you worry about those questions; you are responsible for your team and put them in a bit uncomfortable situation for most of us. But knowing that you want to help the team should give you the nudge you may need to start or continue the reflection sessions.

I was on a panel where psychology students presented their final project work. One group spoke about psychological safety and reflection sessions. While I loved the topic and was impressed by the team's presentation, I asked them whether they applied the concepts in their team. One team member finally spoke up and acknowledged that they had not. I share this story in recognition that the practice is not always easy to start and can feel uncomfortable. But just get started; it usually gets better with practice, as with anything else. After a few reflection meetings, it's worthwhile reflecting upon the sessions themselves to learn.

About What?

The space for board reflection is wide open. As long as reflection helps the individual board members grow, the board as a team to develop, or interactions with management to improve, it serves its purpose. I pointed out before an easy structure for a reflection session after the action. How did we do along with those three categories—outcome, process, and relationship? It is not always evident which category a thought belongs to; therefore, categorization should provide a rough structure. I include a few examples of thoughts that could be mentioned during a reflection session, trying to connect them to a category:

Outcome/Process

Regarding the acquisition, I think we pushed the executive board today to go for a higher price. Is that our role?

Outcome/Process

I did not feel comfortable with today's discussion and decision about the new remuneration system because I sensed that both of you [the Chair and the head of the compensation committee] and the management were tightly aligned. I felt there was no space to ask challenging questions. I could live with the situation if you had framed it as we (the compensation committee and management) had already spent a lot of time on that issue, and that you would be glad that to get that topic approved today. But I felt a bit lost.

Outcome/Relationship

When we decided on that topic, I was not sure if we felt okay as a team. I sensed that something was not on the table. Maybe that would have been a good topic to address quickly, without the management in the private session.

Outcome/Process/Relationship

When we talked about the strategy today, I was a bit lost. Do we know now where the management stands? Where are they insecure?

Process

I am happy with our dividend decision, but I am not pleased with the process. We discussed fine-tuning, not the bigger picture. We should get the bigger picture (outlook for successive years, rough dividend plan, sustainability, alternatives) and spend time on that instead of fine-tuning the micro-decision. I don't know how you felt about that.

Process

When I briefed you today about the audit meeting, I was unsure whether my briefing was too long or too short; it is not the first time I have felt uncertain whether this kind of briefing adds value. Maybe we need a different briefing approach for each committee.

Process

I have the feeling that we are better with concrete decisions, so we like to jump to concrete decisions and fall into the trap of micromanagement.

Process

We should be more precise about what will be presented and just start with questions. We have talked about that several times, but in my opinion, it's not getting better. What can we do?

Relationship

Did we show enough appreciation for the CEO sharing her thoughts concerning the new strategy early on?

Relationship

I just wanted to apologize. You asked a valid question that was not answered in the discussion because I was preoccupied with my thoughts and pushed my point. Please stop me if I do that again.

Relationship

I sensed that you were not happy with that decision, but I didn't want to ask you in the full board meeting. Am I mistaken?

It is also an opportunity to offer praise—specific or more general:

Relationship

I just wanted to thank you for your intervention when Mike and I were becoming a bit wedged together. I appreciate your intervention and how you did it; I felt that you wanted more than just having us stop fighting; you helped us see a different perspective.

I liked the way several of us asked some excellent questions which triggered a good discussion.

Small encouragements can have a significant effect. However, the team has to be cautious not to sugarcoat each other. Once such behavior takes over, it is difficult to address critical issues. If you look at the last two examples, the first one is personal and specific, and the speaker had an active part. The second is not specific and therefore provides less value. You should also be careful not to fall into the trap of allotting grades to everybody, thereby showing your superiority. But if you think your remark is essential, don't be shy in addressing it. Almost nothing is "wrong" as long as you intend to help. You don't have the right intention if you just praise because you want to avoid real topics or wish to be considered the nice guy.

However, I want to point out one pitfall because there is an enormous danger that teams fall into it. *Avoid talking about people who are not present!*

Reflection in groups is a structured approach, directing understanding and learning how to self-regulate in groups. I stress "self-regulation" because it implies group reflection on how you perform as a group. As a general rule, the subject is you-as-a-team. If you are not happy with management's preparation, that should be addressed to management. The risk of board reflection sessions is talking about all possible issues as long as you can avoid talking about yourselves as a team or your feelings within that team. The Chair should clarify the purpose of such a reflection session and intervene if it takes the wrong path. But show patience! The tone and timing of the intervention are a different matter. Maybe a tiny remark at the end fits the purpose better than a schoolmasterly lecture after a board member just spoke up. Sometimes, a board member just needs to vent. A reflection session can have many benefits, but avoid falling into the alluring trap of talking about what management could have done better. The objective is to discuss what *you* can do better.

The session does not serve to collect feedback for the executive board which the Chair will later deliver. Sometimes an issue comes up that you as a board would like to invite the executive board to reflect upon. But obvious points should be addressed directly in the meeting where the executive board can choose to react or digest. This is consistent with an attitude I hold dearly: you should risk something and tell the person directly if you want to criticize something. Using the board's reflection session is a low-risk behavior, which usually does not help improve the working relationship. The Chair should not be a "water carrier" for critical feedback. Naturally, feedback will also emerge on content points to the executive board.

Maybe, as a Chair, you can let your board know that you will ask for points mainly concerning the executive board at the end of the reflection session. With that separation, you can keep the board focused on self-reflection while at the same time offering the opportunity to address something different later.

CHAPTER 11

Reflection Workshop and Board Review

Real change, enduring change, happens one step at a time.
—Ruth Bader Ginsburg

The intuitive mind is a sacred gift, and the rational mind is a faithful servant. We have created a society that honors the servant and has forgotten the gift.
—Albert Einstein

Board Reflection Workshop

Board reflection workshops can have very different content issues depending on the need. Still, they should also serve the purpose of bonding so that you as a team can reflect on your performance in a broader sense than is possible in regular, shorter reflection sessions after the action.

For a successful board reflection workshop, I recommend that you spend about two days together: a board team needs to invest in time to spend together to develop open and trustful relationships. As Schein and Schein (2021) state: "The leap of faith will later allow for greater collective acceleration toward more effective task accomplishment."

I strongly recommend doing such workshops outside of your office premises—preferably in a friendly and cozy environment—where you have time to talk and get to know each other better, essential to developing a board that functions well. We all complain about the unremitting pace of our times, the overflow of information, and not having enough time to reflect. As Daniel Kahneman (2011) said in his book, *Thinking Fast and Slow*, reflective thinking demands slow and deliberate thinking than reactive thinking, which is more action oriented. Fast thinking excludes slow thinking—when one is "on," the other is "off." At least in the western world, our natural inclination is to get things done fast, telling, not inquiring, which runs counter to a reflective environment (Schein and Schein 2021). Some studies claim that brain waves slow down in the natural environment. Slowing down means being more productive for reflection. I am a nature fan anyhow and think a great environment will help the board with such exercises. I also prefer relatively small places, where it is easier to get comfortable quickly, and there is a good likelihood that you will be able to meet independently of the usually fully packed program.

In such a workshop, you may choose to reflect on the strategy or the purpose of the company; it means you can address questions like:

- What is the purpose of the company?
- What would I do differently if I could recreate the company from a blank slate?
- What would I do now if there were no legacy constraints on my actions?
- What do I not know about the industry and the company?

Although the focus may be on business issues, it will also help to develop the relationships as long as you don't fall into the trap of cramming the time with content.

BM: We are doing off-sites with the board and the management, which serve different purposes; mainly, we talk about the future of the business; in doing so, board members and management can interact with each other and get to know each other better. But we always include some exercises where we get more personal and deeper. It helps the bonding.

You can discuss whatever you like as long as it is intended to help individual board members grow, the board develops as a team, or the interactions with the management improve.

You may be in a situation where a new Chair has to be appointed, and the board seizes the opportunity to reflect upon the role of the Chair and the board. It is common to rush to look for the next incumbent, but an organizational role analysis (see Chapter 5) can help create a broader picture. Maybe a nomination committee has done that already and shares its thoughts in such a workshop for the whole board, seeking buy-in for a new role description, or confirming the old one.

Aside from the Chair's role, most boards do not spend sufficient time talking about themselves as a team: What works well, where we can improve, what is our role? A lot is taken for granted, unsaid, untouched. It is easier to leave things unchanged in a part-time job. However, if you are serious about the board as a team, you should take your time and reflect upon questions such as in Figure 11.1.

Potential Reflection Topics

- What is the role of the Chair?
- What is the role of the board?
- What can we improve to ensure that the committee work is meaningful for the full board?
- What expectations do I have and are those aligned with the expectations of the others?
- How might I contribute to the board?
- How do I support or hinder management progress?
- What are my concerns and fears?
- What am I/are we avoiding?
- What do I need in order to show the desired behavior?

Figure 11.1 Potential reflection topics

Why Board Evaluation?

I favor the board's reflective attitude, and I favor board evaluation: Is this a contradiction? No, reflection is a must; an evaluation is an input that provides food for thought, makes reflection easier, and may point out issues that won't come up without an evaluation.

BM: The board evaluation allows us to have a dialogue about issues that otherwise do not surface.

BM: One of the values of these board reviews is that you learn things you thought you were doing okay, but the other's perception is not quite your perception.

BM: We conduct board reviews and take the time for extensive workshops to discuss elephants in the room and reflect on ourselves. This led to me being less directive which helps the team.

BM: During the board review, the question arose [about] how I am getting along with the CEO. I thought I had communicated that I have some issues with her, but the question proved that I hadn't been entirely clear enough.

BM: We just had an external board review, and one of their suggestions was that we should have one of these little cards on how we expect meetings to be conducted (contents to be determined, all views welcome, open debate encouraged, etc.). I was pretty surprised by that because it had never particularly occurred to me that was necessary; this board is small, has good people, and everybody speaks and debates, so I was surprised that they expressed the need for such a card.

Board evaluation is a tool that helps get the reflection process started by getting input material. The "exact" results of that input are secondary. It is not science; the purpose is to direct you to topics and stimulate reflection. If I refer to board evaluation here, I do not talk about the more formal reviews focusing on legal requirements; rather, it is a discussion about improving the team's performance, focusing on behaviors. If I declare the board evaluation's primary function to be input for the reflection session, it is clear that board evaluation in no way replaces reflection. The two biggest dangers of board evaluations are the wrong focus on formal issues and evaluations with a mindset of confirming that all is good, avoiding reflection altogether.

Board Survey, Interviews, Observation—Use the Board Members as the Primary Tool

Who knows more about the board than the board members themselves? I strongly encourage boards to reflect upon themselves and use each board member and their collective intelligence and intuition as a resource.

Using *self-report surveys* is efficient and offers easy access to board members' thoughts, feelings, and concerns. The act of answering the questions should promote greater self-awareness and thereby open the door to self-development. An easy and commonly used scale for the questions is 1 to 5 (strongly agree to disagree strongly). More critical, provide ample space to provide comments at the end of each question.

The comments are often more helpful than the numerical compilation of the results. And above all, include open questions, which allow thoughts to be triggered and collected that otherwise might not come to light. Appendix 1 includes a regular board review survey which I drafted as a model for you to edit according to your needs.

Although a survey is a relatively simple matter for collecting thoughts, I recommend adding *semistructured interviews*. Interviews give you a very different taste of what is going on and what should be addressed and avoided.

Input can also come from observing the board:

BM: We allow external support to observe board meetings. It was not undisputed, but we had good experiences.

I have observed boards, and indeed it can be beneficial and insightful. My dream scenario would be to do all three—survey, interviews, and observation. It shows you a lot. But I understand a certain reluctance, and I am not sure if the dynamics differ. If I had to give up one, it would be sitting in a meeting. Observing can lead to the board deciding to call in an expert; neither the expert nor the board should fall into that trap. Board members themselves are the primary tool to be used in sharing insights about how the board can develop to do even better.

Board Evaluation With External Support

If observation is a part of a board evaluation, it is a given that you need external support. Sometimes, the Chair or the Vice-Chair will lead interviews to collect thoughts for the workshop. While I fully support the more extensive talks between the Chair and the board members throughout the year (see Chapter 5), I favor using external support for a survey and, in particular, for the interviews for a variety of reasons.

BM: Recently, we had an expert who conducted the survey, did the interviews, and observed two regular board meetings; that was very helpful and provided more weight.

Somebody has to compile the information. Perhaps the secretary of the board has such a neutral and trustworthy position. I would not recommend the Chair doing it. His role is too crucial in the overall process. As a former secretary of the board, I sometimes had that task. But our survey at that time—while providing open space—dealt more with technical issues (preparation of meetings, length, topics) and had no focus on addressing the psychodynamic issues on the board. So the task at that time was doable. The more you lean into how you interact with each other, the more an independent third-party professional is needed. Without the neutrality and the critical challenge of an external board coach, the board will have a tendency to confirm that it is performing as expected. Leaving the comfort zone comes not naturally for a board or as Toya Lorch (Brissett, Sher, and Smith 2020) puts it nicely: "Most board members have reached a certain stage in their careers where they live in an environment that is not conducive to self-development."

Board coaches should have extensive board experiences of their own to get the necessary acceptance and to make it easier to crystallize essential points.

However, the third-party professional should be a self-aware and reflective person as well in order not to push their views in the interview process. The third-party should focus on collecting and listening. The interviews, therefore, should be structured but not followed rigidly. The external party can, by all means, provide feedback, but their main job is to set the ground for the board's reflection sessions. If the board takes the reflection seriously, it will make a big difference in their readiness to accept and adapt if the board comes to certain conclusions on their own (supported by data) compared to a third party telling the board what to do. But it makes a difference if you have a neutral person to collect and condense the data and run that part of the workshop. The central role of the Chair is just too crucial to run the workshop as well. In some companies, the Vice-Chair runs the evaluation.

BM: The board assesses me without me being present; the Vice-Chair takes over.

While this can work, the Vice-Chair usually is quite close to the Chair, which has its advantages but makes an evaluation less neutral; it can be questionable how open the board members will be with the Vice-Chair. I also like the Chair being included in the entire reflection session—leaving the stage has implications of formality.

Provide the Executive Board the Chance to Give You Feedback

I have stressed taking the board as the primary resource and having an expert who does not need to be center stage. However, I strongly recommend giving the executive board the chance to provide input and feedback. Reflection and feedback in an executive board are already rare. Still, they have the board of directors who—as part of its task—control the management, decide upon their remuneration, and hopefully provide feedback. However, who provides feedback for the board of directors? To quote Sonnenfeld (2002): "I can't think of a single workgroup whose performance gets assessed less rigorously than corporate boards."

As we have seen earlier, the executive board is often somewhat skeptical about the board. Therefore, the executive board should have the opportunity to speak up. Speaking up means that the executive board can reflect upon what the board could do better. Shift them from complaining about the board and feeling like a victim to becoming active players with the chance of addressing their concerns. It can also help them to vent. But most importantly, to provide valuable feedback to the board, management should also see the board's perspective. This will help them better understand the board, and it provides feedback or input for the board reflection.

> *BM: I keep hearing management from other companies complaining about the board. I dare to say—not with us. We do an assessment every year with feedback from the executive committee to the board of directors. Everyone can say what they like, what bothers them, and so on. It helps us a lot, and sometimes we can even laugh together.*

Feedback from the executive board should be an annual, formalized process. I also include a short survey in Appendix 2 which can be used for the executive board; you may add short interviews—at least for the CEO.

I suggest combining the input from the board's self-evaluation with the picture you get from the executive board for your reflection workshop.

Focus on the Team Instead of Individual Evaluations

Beatty (2012) calls for peer evaluation. The purpose is to provide help rather than hurting your peers. A possible scale is "needs improvement," "perfectly adequate," and "outstanding." I am personally skeptical about the focus on individuals and the rating system.

> BM: We rate each other and then look at the numbers, but I think it is a paper exercise. We should talk to each other and reflect together instead of focusing on the rating.

The intention might be clear and reasonable; the outcome might be perceived differently and depends heavily on cultures. According to a study by Cloyd, Keller and DeNicola (2012), 97.8 percent of boards are engaged in some form of board evaluation process; however, the focus is on the individual rather than the team. While we are expected to rate ourselves too highly, the team scores in a study by Heidrick and Struggles (2010) were three times worse than the individual self-scores. In line with Charas (2015), I recommend that boards replace individual evaluations of board members with a team-based assessment.

> BM: I don't want to have individual ratings of board members except for me as Chair. More harm than benefit.

As this Chair points out, the Chair has to be an exception because he stands out with his role; a review could also cover questions about the committee's heads, but the focus overall should be on the *team*— consistent with the significance of teams in today's business world.

Peer Talks Instead of Peer Evaluation

An easy way to get peers to talk about each other is through peer talks and walks. I had good experiences with peer talks where you spend, for example, 20 minutes and share some observations about the other person and vice versa. Starting with something appreciative often helps. Even if you believe that it's something the other person is aware of, hearing it makes a difference. I once said to a CFO with whom I frequently had opposing views that I appreciated his down-to-earth attitude and that he was not a gambler. For his role, it makes a difference and provides trust. The CFO seemed touched by my comment, which I thought at the time was quite evident.

Don't just focus on what a person should avoid. It should be the other way around. Peer talks can be easily included in a workshop and combined with a short walk, allowing participants to stretch their legs and get fresh air. Walking together in the same direction also has a less formal feel and a different symbolism than a setting where you sit opposite each other.

Summary

An old proverb says that all roads lead to Rome. I would add a qualification, as long as we have an open attitude toward exploring and learning. This is particularly true for boards whose framework and the stage of the career of their members do not readily support an approach of curiosity and learning.

There is no simple rule book to human beings, or anything that includes human behaviour; so I would be the last person to pretend that elevating the performance of the board is as simple, or mechanical, as following some kind of check list. But there are some general truths that we have explored that I believe can make all the difference in creating and running an effective board.

Acknowledge that a board is a team with needs. If we are willing to improve board teams' functioning, we need to acknowledge that a board is a social entity—a team—that has to be treated as such. Each person on such a team has needs like belonging, inclusion, and safety, which must be attended to.

Take time to form a team. What seems familiar today to management teams is not yet the norm for board teams, even though the awareness that boards need to manage board dynamics issues and act as a team is rapidly increasing.

Create a safe space, encourage sharing vulnerability and speaking up. Experience and research have taught us that we need to feel psychologically safe and nurtured if we are to commit. Then we can engage in debates and can share vulnerability.

Talk about your roles and concerns. The delicate position of boards—between the Chair and the executive team—makes it awkward for them to define their task and role. It is convenient and comfortable to slide into a rather passive attitude, with the justification that management runs, and the Chair takes good care of, the company. Boards are still reluctant to talk about their role, address the more personal and hidden topics, and accept that conflicts are part of the job if they take their work seriously.

Create a learning atmosphere and learn to tolerate uncertainty. Boards' self-concept, growing task complexity, and increasing diversity will require that they put more emphasis on the human side of their job. Boards need self-esteem to be open for learning: to question how things have been done in the past, to tolerate uncertainty and endure ambiguity, and finally also to challenge themselves with the aim to grow.

Board members and in particular the Chair need great people skills. In creating such a learning or coaching environment, the Chair plays a central role. The Chair's role is in the background, not center stage, with a willingness to be a team player and to form a team. His attitude is mainly supportive, sometimes challenging and nudging and, if needed, setting clear boundaries. This asks for reflective personalities so strong that they do not need to demonstrate that strength most of the time. The questions remain who can help the Chair perform well and who is able to nudge and develop the Chair. Any Chair is well advised to have people on his board and in his surroundings who are not shy about addressing critical issues and providing honest feedback.

Acknowledge emotions and build relationships of high trust and openness. Boards and top management are roaming in a web of complex relations. In management circles, strength is often shown through dominating behavior and not allowing insecurities to be voiced. We act and pretend as if we always have the answers, but our only chance of success is to build it together. This asks for a mindset shift in management inconsistent with the image of heroes at the top. It is one of assuming and knowing less, asking more, and building bridges. It is connecting the dots, especially the human dots. The interviews I conducted showed a wide variety of ways of navigating the human side of board relationships, from being purely focused on tasks and leaving emotions aside, to cautiously opening up or even courageously addressing them. According to Schein (2021), "maintaining professional distance is not particularly helpful" if we know that we need to collaborate in order to be successful. It may be counterintuitive, but "to build and reinforce relationship of high trust and openness" may be the most important thing to learn.

The key relationship is between the Chair and the CEO; they have to invest time to work on their relationship; they need to learn to ask questions and to share their needs to have a relationship based on mutual trust. Open and transparent communication is a must for a flourishing relationship between the Chair and CEO. Both have also to manage their relationships within and between their teams. The web of relationships is clouded by functions, hierarchy, prestige, and power. We are well advised not to take it for granted that these relationships will naturally prosper in such a complex environment.

Developing trusting and open relationships is only possible if board members are willing to take certain personal risks; if boards do not take the risk of revealing themselves and their vulnerability or entering into debates for the company's sake, they will find it difficult to improve their performance; they have to be ready to tackle the more personal issues of working together.

Conduct joint reflections. Joint reflections are one great tool to make board rooms better. They can provide the necessary psychological safety and a feeling of belonging. The board members themselves are the board's best reflection machine, but have to be actively steered, and benefit from different input sources like the executive board's feedback and appropriate external support.

> *BM: To have an open dialogue in a group of about 10 grownup people, most with a successful history, is a great challenge, and it is also important not to leave this to chance but to promote it in a targeted way. Since we have been assessing ourselves, jointly reflecting upon the input, and have also condensed and sharpened our insights through an external third party, I have already experienced a perceptible change in the discussion culture here on the board of directors.*

If board members feel included, get to know each other, and share private issues; are engaged and perceive encouragement to speak up, enter into debates, and manage conflicts; and reflect upon themselves, then your board has a great chance of being a great team, having fruitful dialogues to the company's benefit.

Our feelings and emotions are often the root cause of relationship issues; we should learn to sense them, reflect upon them, and talk about them instead of suppressing them. This needs courage—especially in an environment where our appearance and reputation are crucial. However, asking about the concerns of others and acknowledging our own allows us to foster better relationships for our and the company's well-being. At the same time, it makes us more human.

APPENDIX 1

Board Members' Self-Survey for Board Evaluation

Except if stated otherwise, the response format is: strongly disagree, disagree, neither agree nor disagree, agree, strongly agree.

Board

Structure, Composition, Role Clarity, Meetings

I am satisfied with the size of the board.

The board has the best composition of skills and experience to meet the needs of the company.

We share a common understanding of the board's role.

We share a common understanding of the Chair's function.

We share a common understanding of the committee's work.

I believe I have sufficient access to management and company employees.

Our board is very effective.

Our board regularly evaluates the skills and capabilities of directors to ensure that the board and the committees are chaired and staffed effectively.

The agendas cover topics that are relevant to the board.

Major Topics

I believe I have a sufficient understanding of company strategy.

I believe I have a sufficient understanding of the major risks faced by our company.

The board is actively involved in its succession planning.

The board has a succession plan in place for the Chair.

The board has a succession plan in place for the CEO.

I believe I have a good understanding of the talent pipeline and possible successors to the executive board.

Board Dialogue and Team

How Would You Rate Your Board for the Following Dimensions?
(Response format: very much; somewhat; not at all)

Onboarding new directors
Inviting the active participation of all directors
Expressing different points of view openly and sincerely
Listening to the views of others
Questioning each other when we think the work can be done better
Bringing up problems and tough issues
Tolerating dissent
Leveraging the skills of all board members
Asking the right questions
Understanding the strategy
Challenging management
Sharing relevant information
Sharing private issues
Making room to get to know each other
Being open to new points of view
Having a high level of trust among board members
Being open to self-disclosure
Providing direct, personal, and constructive feedback to fellow directors
Reflecting together about the role and concerns of the board

How Would You Rate Yourself Among Those Dimensions?
(Response format: very much; somewhat; not at all)

Listen well.
Raise questions.
Independent.
Build on the others' contributions.

Hold others accountable.

Earn trust.

Demonstrate humility and empathy.

To What Extent Do You Believe the Following Are a Problem on Your Board?

Board members allow personal or past experience to dominate their perspective.

Board members do not express their point of view when management is present.

Board members are too quick to reach a consensus.

Board members do not encourage dissenting views.

Board members do not understand the boundary between oversight and actively trying to manage the company.

Board members derail the conversation by introducing off-topic items.

Board members are distracted by technology during meetings.

Board members are not prepared for meetings.

Some board members have an outsized influence on the board's decision.

Our board is NOT very effective at bringing in new talent to refresh the board's capabilities.

Management Interaction

I am satisfied with the quality, length, and depth of the prereads.

I believe management presents realistically and the assumptions and risks are highlighted.

The board serves as a sounding board for the CEO.

The CEO and his team share risks or bad news openly with the board.

Management informs the board on all essential matters and communicates openly.

Management is sufficiently responsive to questions and issues raised by the board.

The board sufficiently challenges management.

The board sufficiently supports management.

The board and the management have a trustworthy and open working relationship.

The board and the management have each a good understanding of their respective roles.

Committee

I am satisfied with the board's current committee structure.

I am satisfied with how we rotate committee members.

I am satisfied with the succession planning of the committees.

For Each Committee

The committee has the best composition of skills and experience to meet the needs of a company.

I am satisfied with the performance of the_____ committee.

I am satisfied with the reporting and feedback of the audit committee to the entire board.

We share a common role understanding of the committee.

Chair

The Chair encourages trust among board members and a collaborative culture.

The Chair ensures high-quality debates within the board, encouraging different viewpoints in the discussions.

The Chair helps us develop as a team.

The Chair ensures a good balance between time for presentations, discussions, decisions, and reflection.

The Chair is able to set boundaries if necessary.

The Chair is a reflective person and open to self-disclosure.

The Chair promotes effective relationships and communication between the board members.

The Chair is open for contacts between board members and the management team.

Open Questions

In my opinion, the top strategic and operational issues for the board are:

In which of the following areas (strategy, finance, people, corporate culture, operative performance, innovation, risks, competition, regulation, compliance, reflection) or not listed areas, the board should spend:

More time:

Less time:

In my personal opinion, the board is doing very well in the following areas:

In my personal opinion, the board has improved in the following areas:

In my personal opinion, the board could handle the following better:

The following topics/issues, related to my position as a board member and the board's performance, worry me the most:

Any specific remark to one of the questions?

A question which was missing?

Any other comments?

Thank you!

APPENDIX 2

Survey for Management's Input for Board Review

The executive board is referred to as "Mgt" and the board of directors as "BoD." The response format is: very much; somewhat; not much.

General Questions

The BoD understands our challenges.

The BoD understands our strategy.

The BoD gives us sufficient leeway.

The BoD is a sparring partner.

Working with the BoD is a benefit for Mgt.

The work with the committees is a benefit for Mgt.

BoD and Mgt Interactions

The BoD serves as a sounding board for Mgt.

The BoD and the Mgt have a trustworthy and open working relationship.

The BoD has a good understanding of the role of Mgt.

The BoD sufficiently challenges mgt.

The BoD sufficiently supports mgt.

Mgt has a good understanding of the role of the BoD.

Mgt openly shares risks or bad news with the BoD.

Mgt informs the BoD on all important matters and communicates openly.

Mgt is sufficiently responsive to questions and issues raised by the BoD.

I am satisfied with the quality, length, and depth of our prereads to the BoD.

I believe we realistically present, and the assumptions and risks are clearly highlighted.

I believe that we show our vulnerabilities by disclosing where we are uncertain.

Open Questions

In my opinion, the top strategic and operational issues for the BoD are:

In which of the following areas (strategy, finance, people, corporate culture, operative performance, innovation, risks, competition, regulation, compliance, reflection) or not listed areas:

the BoD should spend more time:

the BoD should spend less time:

In my personal opinion, the BoD is doing very well in the following areas:

In my personal opinion, the BoD has improved in the following areas:

In my personal opinion, the BoD could have handled the following matters better:

Any specific remark to one of the questions?

Any missing questions?

Any other comments?

Thank you!

References

Argyris, C. 1991. "Teaching Smart People How to Learn." *Harvard Business Review* 69, no. 3, pp. 4–15.

Avery, G.C. 2004. *Understanding Leadership: Paradigm and Cases.* Thousand Oaks, CA: Sage.

Bacharach, S.B., P. Bamberger, and V. McKinney. 2000. "Boundary Management Tactics and Logics of Action: The Case of Peer-Support Providers." *Administrative Science Quarterly* 45, no. 4, pp. 704–736.

Beatty, D.R. 2012. "The Role of the Chair Orchestrating the Board." *Rotman Magazine*, pp. 48–53. Spring.

Bergmann, B., and J. Schaeppi. 2016. "A Data-Driven Approach to Group Creativity." *Harvard Business Review* 12, pp. 43–62.

BlackRock. January 2019. "Investment Stewardship's Approach to Engagement on Long-Term Strategy, Purpose, and Culture." Available from www.blackrock.com/corporate/literature/publication/blk-commentary-engaging-on-strategy-purpose-culture.pdf

Bogusz, A. 2013. *Reflective Work in the Workplace—Mirror, Mirror on the Wall—How Much Do I Really Want to See?* [Thesis]. Fontainebleau: INSEAD EMCCC.

Braun, S. 2017. "Leader Narcissism and Outcomes in Organizations: A Review at Multiple Levels of Analysis and Implications for Future Research." *Frontiers in Psychology* 8, no. 773, pp. 1–22. https://doi.org/10.3389/fpsyg.2017.00773

Bregman, P. 2013. "Nine Practices to Help You Say No." *Harvard Business Review* (digital article). Available from https://hbr.org/2013/02/nine-practices-to-help-you-say

Bresó, I., F.J. Gracia, F. Latorre, and J.M. Peiró. 2008. "Development and Validation of the Team Learning Questionnaire." *Comportamento Organizacional e Gestão* 14, no. 2, pp. 145–160.

Bridges, W., and S. Bridges. 2016. *Managing Transitions: Making the Most of Change.* Boston, MA: Da Capo Press.

Brissett, L., M. Sher, and T.L. Smith, eds. 2020. *Dynamics at Boardroom Level: A Tavistock Primer for Leaders, Coaches and Consultants.* New York, NY: Routledge.

Brown, B. 2018. *Dare to Lead: Brave Work. Tough Conversations. Whole Hearts.* New York, NY: Random House.

Burris, E.R. 2012. "The Risks and Rewards of Speaking Up: Managerial Responses to Employee Voice." *Academy of Management Journal* 55, no. 4, pp. 851–875.

Cannon, T. 1996. *Welcome to the Revolution: Managing Paradox in the 21st Century*. London: Pitman.

Charan, R., D. Carey, and M. Useem. 2013. *Boards That Lead: When to Take Charge, When to Partner, and When to Stay Out of the Way*. Harvard Business Review Press.

Charas, S. 2015. "Improving Corporate Performance by Enhancing Team Dynamics at the Board Level." *International Journal of Disclosure and Governance* 12, no. 2, pp. 107–131.

Cloyd, M.A., D. Keller, and P. DeNicola. 2012. "PWC's 2012 Annual Corporate Directors Survey." Center for Board Governance. Available from www. pwc.com/us/en/corporate-governance/ publications/boardroom-direct-newsletter/ september-2012-issues-in-brief.jhtml

Cramer, P. (2012). *The development of defense mechanisms: Theory, research, and assessment*. Springer Science & Business Media.

Covey, S.R., and S. Covey. 2020. *The 7 Habits of Highly Effective People*. UK: Simon & Schuster.

Covey, S.R., and R.R. Merrill. 2006. *The Speed of Trust: The One Thing That Changes Everything*. Simon & Schuster.

Dalton, D.R., C.M. Daily, A.E. Ellstrand, and J.L. Johnson. 1998. "Meta-Analytic Reviews of Board Composition, Leadership Structure, and Financial Performance." *Strategic Management Journal* 19, no. 3, pp. 269–290.

Detert, J.R., and E.R. Burris. 2007. "Leadership Behavior and Employee Voice: Is the Door Really Open?" *Academy of Management Journal* 50, no. 4, pp. 869–884.

Detert, J.R., and A.C. Edmondson. 2011. "Implicit Voice Theories: Taken-for-Granted Rules of Self-Censorship at Work." *Academy of Management Journal* 54, no. 3, pp. 461–488.

Detert, J.R., and L.K. Treviño. 2010. "Speaking Up to Higher-Ups: How Supervisors and Skip-Level Leaders Influence Employee Voice." *Organization Science* 21, no. 1, pp. 249–270.

Dignan, A. 2019. *Brave New Work: Are You Ready to Reinvent Your Organization?* London: Penguin.

Drucker, P.F. 2010. *HBR's 10 Must Reads on Managing Yourself*. Boston, MA: Harvard Business School Publishing Corporation.

Duhigg, C. 2016. "What Google Learned from its Quest to Build the Perfect Team." *The New York Times Magazine* 26. Available from www.nytimes. com/2016/02/28/magazine/what-google-learned-from-its-quest-to-build-the-perfect-team.html

Dunne, P. 2019. *Boards, A Practical Perspective*. London: Governance Publishing.

Edmondson, A.C. 1999. "Psychological Safety and Learning Behavior in Work Teams." *Administrative Science Quarterly* 44, no. 2, pp. 350–383.

Edmondson, A.C. 2012. *Teaming: How Organizations Learn, Innovate, and Compete in the Knowledge Economy*. San Francisco, CA: John Wiley & Sons.

Edmondson, A.C. 2018. *The Fearless Organization: Creating Psychological Safety in the Workplace for Learning, Innovation, and Growth*. John Wiley & Sons.

Edmondson, A.C., and Z. Lei. 2014. "Psychological Safety: The History, Renaissance, and Future of an Interpersonal Construct." *Annual Review of Organizational Psychology and Organizational Behavior* 1, no. 1, pp. 23–43.

Edmondson, A.C., and D.M. Smith. 2006. "Too Hot to Handle? How to Manage Relationship Conflict." *California Management Review* 49, no. 1, pp. 6–31.

Engbers, M.J.E. 2020. *How the Unsaid Shapes Decision-Making in Boards: A Reflexive Exploration of Paradigms in the Boardroom* [Thesis]. Vrije Universitet Amsterdam).

Ethos. 2018. "Proxy Voting Guidelines, Corporate Governance Principles." Available from www.ethosfund.ch/sites/default/files/201712/LDPCG_Ethos_2018_EN_FINAL.pdf

Fama, E.F., and M.C. Jensen. 1983. "Separation of Ownership and Control." *The Journal of Law and Economics* 26, no. 2, pp. 301–325.

Farjoun, M. 2010. "Beyond Dualism: Stability and Change as a Duality." *Academy of Management Review* 35, no. 2, pp. 202–225.

Finkelstein, S., and D. Hambrick. 1996. *Strategic Leadership*. St. Paul, MN: West Educational Publishing.

Finkelstein, S., and A.C. Mooney. 2003. "Not the Usual Suspects: How to Use Board Process to Make Boards Better." *The Academy of Management Executive* 17, no. 2, pp. 101–113.

Forbes, D.P., and F.J. Milliken. 1999. "Cognition and Corporate Governance: Understanding Boards of Directors as Strategic Decision-Making Groups." *Academy of Management Review* 24, no. 3, pp. 489–505.

Frazier, M.L., S. Fainshmidt, R.L. Klinger, A. Pezeshkan, and V. Vracheva. 2017. "Psychological Safety: A Meta-Analytic Review and Extension." *Personnel Psychology* 70, no. 1, pp. 113–165.

Fredberg, T. 2014. "If I Say It's Complex, It Bloody Well Will Be: CEO Strategies for Managing Paradox." *Journal of Applied Behavioral Science* 50, no. 2, pp. 171–188.

Gallo, A. 2017. *HBR Guide to Dealing with Conflict (HBR Guide Series)*. Harvard Business Review Press.

Garvin, D.A., and M.A. Roberto. 2001. "What You Don't Know About Making Decisions." *Harvard Business Review* 79, no. 8, pp. 108–119.

Geertshuis, S.A., R.L. Morrison, and H.D. Cooper-Thomas. 2015. "It's Not What You Say, It's the Way That You Say It: The Mediating Effect of Upward Influencing Communications on the Relationship Between Leader-Member

Exchange and Performance Ratings." *International Journal of Business Communication* 52, no. 2, pp. 228–245.

Gershfeld, L., and R. Sedehi. 2021. *Emotional Connection: The EmC Strategy: How Leaders Can Unlock the Human Potential, Build Resilient Teams, and Nurture Thriving Cultures.* Business Expert Press.

Giles, S. 2016. "The Most Important Leadership Competencies, According to Leaders Around the World." *Harvard Business Review* 15, no. 3.

Goleman, D., R. Boyatzis, and A. McKee. 2001. "Primal Leadership: The Hidden Driver of Great Performance." *Harvard Business Review* 79, no. 11, pp. 42–53.

Goleman, D., E. Langer, C. Congleton, and A. McKee. 2017. *Harvard Business Review Emotional Intelligence Collection*, 4 vols. Harvard Business Review Press.

Greenberg, J., and M.S. Edwards. 2009. *Voice and Silence in Organizations.* Emerald Group Publishing.

Griffin, T., D.F. Larcker, S. Miles, and B. Tayan. 2017. "Board Evaluations and Boardroom Dynamics, Rock Center for Corporate Governance at Stanford University Closer Look Series: Topics, Issues and Controversies in Corporate Governance No. CGRP63." *Stanford University Graduate School of Business Research Paper*, pp. 17–22.

Hackman, J.R. 2009. "Why Teams Don't Work. Interview by Diane Coutu." *Harvard Business Review* 87, no. 5, pp. 98–105.

Hambrick, D.C. 2007. "Upper Echelons Theory: An Update." *Academy of Management Review* 32, no. 2, pp. 334–343.

Heidrick and Struggles. 2010. *USC and Heidrick and Struggles' Board Director Survey: Achieving the Perfect CEO-Board Dynamic.* Marshall School Center for Effective Organizations.

Heifetz, R.A., A. Grashow, and M. Linsky. 2009. *The Practice of Adaptive Leadership: Tools and Tactics for Changing Your Organization and the World.* Boston, MA: Harvard Business Press.

Helwig, P. 1967. "Das Wertequadrat." *Psyche* 2, no. 1, pp. 121–127.

Hirschhorn, L., and T. Gilmore. 1992. "The New Boundaries of the 'Boundaryless' Company." *Harvard Business Review* 70, no. 3, pp. 104–115.

Hirschhorn, L. 1990. *The workplace within: Psychodynamics of organizational life* (Vol. 8). MIT press.

Ibarra, H. 2015. "The Authenticity Paradox." *Harvard Business Review* 93, nos. 1/2, pp. 53–59.

Jackman, J.M., and M.H. Strober. 2003. "Fear of Feedback." *Harvard Business Review* 81, no. 4, pp. 101–108.

James, W. 1890. "The Perception of Reality." *Principles of Psychology* 2, pp. 283–324.

Janis, I. 1982. *Groupthink.* 2nd ed. Boston, MA: Houghton Miffin.

Jensen, M.C., and W.H. Meckling. 1976. "Theory of the Firm: Managerial Behavior, Agency Costs and Ownership Structure." *Journal of Financial Economics* 3, no. 4, pp. 305–360.

Johnson, S.G., K. Schnatterly, and A.D. Hill. 2013. "Board Composition Beyond Independence: Social Capital, Human Capital, and Demographics." *Journal of Management* 39, no. 1, pp. 232–262.

Kahneman, D. 2011. *Thinking, Fast and Slow*. Macmillan.

Kakabadse, A. and N. Kakabadse. 2008. *Leading the Board: The Six Disciplines of World-Class Chairmen*. Palgrave.

Kalss, S. 2020. "Aufsichtsrat und Verwaltugsrat: in Network for Innovative Corporate Governance 2020/1, Board Dynamics, Future of Governance Management." Universität St.Gallen. Available from https://static1. squarespace.com/static/5c6bca3f0b77bde28679d229/t/6064e5f7d3b588 0468a12335/1617225207735/NICG_2020-1_Kalss_final.pdf

Kayes D.C. 2017. "The Limits and Consequences of Experience Absent Reflection: Implications for Learning and Organizing." In *Organizing Reflection*, pp. 79–94. Routledge.

Kegan, R., L. Lahey, A. Fleming, and M. Miller. 2014. "Making Business Personal." *Harvard Business Review* 92, no. 4, pp. 44–52.

Keltner, D. 2016. *The Power Paradox: How We Gain and Lose Influence*. Penguin.

Kets de Vries, M.F.R. January 2004. "Putting Leaders on the Couch: A Conversation with Manfred F. R. Kets de Vries." Harvard Business Review, 1–8. Available from www.hbr.org

Kets de Vries, M.F.R. 2006. *The Leadership Mystique: Leading Behavior in the Human Enterprise*. Pearson Education.

Kets de Vries, M.F.R. 2011. *The Hedgehog Effect: The Secrets of Building High Performance Teams*. John Wiley & Sons.

Kets de Vries, M.F.R. 2014a. "The Psycho-Path to Disaster Coping with SOB Executives." *Organizational Dynamics* 43, pp. 17–26.

Kets de Vries, M.F.R. 2014b. "Coaching the Toxic Leader." *Harvard Business Review*. Magazine article. Available from https://hbr.org/2014/04/coaching-the-toxic-leader?autocomplete=true

Kets de Vries, M.F.R. 2017. "How to Manage a Narcissist." *Harvard Business Review*. Available from https://hbr.org/2017/05/how-to-manage-a-narcissist

Kets de Vries, M.F.R., and A. Cheak. 2014. *Psychodynamic Approach*. INSEAD Working paper, 2014/45/EFE. Available from https://papers.ssrn.com/sol3/papers.cfm?abstract_id=2456594

Kline, N. 1999. *Time to Think: Listening to Ignite the Human Mind*. Hachette UK.

Krantz, J. 2010. "Social Defences and Twenty-First Century Organizations." *British Journal of Psychotherapy* 26, no. 2, pp. 192–201.

Lambrechts, F.J., R. Bouwen, S. Grieten, J.P. Huybrechts, and E.H. Schein. 2011. "Learning to Help Through Humble Inquiry and Implications for Management Research, Practice, and Education: An Interview with Edgar. H. Schein." *Academy of Management Learning & Education* 10, no. 1, pp. 131–147.

Lawrence, B.S. 1997. "Perspective—The Black Box of Organizational Demography." *Organization Science* 8, no. 1, pp. 1–22.

Lencioni, P.M. 2002. *The Five Dysfunctions of a Team.* Jossey-Bass.

Lencioni, P.M. 2016. *The Ideal Team Player: How to Recognize and Cultivate the Three Essential Virtues.* John Wiley & Sons.

Lewis, M.W. 2000. "Exploring Paradox: Toward a More Comprehensive Guide." *Academy of Management Review* 25, no. 4, pp. 760–776.

Long, S. 2018. "Drawing From Role Biography in Organizational Role Analysis." In *Coaching in Depth: The Organizational Role Analysis Approach*, eds. S. Long, J. Newton, and B. Sievers, 125–144. Routledge.

Lyubomirsky, S., and H.S. Lepper. 1999. "A Measure of Subjective Happiness: Preliminary Reliability and Construct Validation." *Social Indicators Research* 46, no. 2, pp. 137–155.

Maccoby, M. 2004. "Narcissistic Leaders: The Incredible Pros, the Inevitable Cons." *Harvard Business Review* 82, no. 1, p. 92.

Mace, M.L. 1971. *Directors: Myth and Reality.* Boston, MA: Harvard University Graduate School of Business Administration.

Mayo, M. 2018. *Yours Truly: Staying Authentic in Leadership and Life.* Bloomsbury Publishing.

Meyer, E. 2014. *The Culture Map: Breaking Through the Invisible Boundaries of Global Business.* New York, NY: Public Affairs.

Milgram, S., 1974. *Obedience to Authority.* New York, NY: Harper and Row.

Mlodinow, L. 2013. *Subliminal: How Your Unconscious Mind Rules Your Behavior.* New York, NY: Vintage Books.

Morais, F., A. Kakabadse, and N. Kakabadse. 2018. "The Chairperson and CEO Roles' Interaction and Responses to Strategic Tensions." *Corporate Governance: The International Journal of Business in Society* 18, no. 1, pp. 143–164. Available from https://doi.org/10.1108/CG-05-2017-0092

Morrison, E.W. 2014. "Employee Voice and Silence." *Annual Review of Organizational Psychology and Organizational Behavior* 1, no. 1, pp. 173–197.

Morrison, E.W., and F.J. Milliken. 2000. "Organizational Silence: A Barrier to Change and Development in a Pluralistic World." *Academy of Management Review* 25, no. 4, pp. 706–725.

Newman, A., R. Donohue, and N. Eva. 2017. "Psychological Safety: A Systematic Review of the Literature." *Human Resource Management Review* 27, no. 3, pp. 521–53.

Pettigrew, A. 1992. "On Studying Managerial Elites." *Strategic Management Journal* 13, pp. 163–182.

Pomin, F. 2019. *Surviving Narcissistic Leadership* [Thesis]. Fontainebleau: INSEAD EMCCC.

Porter, J. 2017. "Why You Should Make Time for Self-Reflection (Even If You Hate Doing It)." *Harvard Business Review (Digital Article)*. Available from https://hbr.org/2017/03/why-you-should-make-time-for-self-reflection-even-if-you-hate-doing-it

Prudential Regulation Authority of the Bank of England. July 2018. *Strengthening Individual Accountability in Banking*. Supervisory Statement, SS28/15.

Quinn, R.E. 2005. "Moments of Greatness." *Harvard Business Review* 83, nos. 7/8, pp. 74–83.

Riemann F. 1961. *Grundformen der Angst und die Antinomien des Lebens*. München-Basel, Ernst-Reinhardt Verlag.

Robbins, M. 2019. "Why Employees Need Both Recognition and Appreciation." *Harvard Business Review*. Available from https://hbr.org/2019/11/why-employees-need-both-recognition-and-appreciation

Roberts, J. 2002. "Building the Complementary Board. The Work of the Plc Chairman." *Long Range Planning* 35, no. 5, pp. 493–520.

Roberts, J., T. McNulty, and P. Stiles. 2005. "Beyond Agency Conceptions of the Work of the Non-Executive Director: Creating Accountability in the Boardroom." *British Journal of Management* 16, pp. S5–S26.

Robertson, B.J. 2016. *Holacracy: Ein revolutionäres Management-System für eine volatile Welt*. Vahlen.

Rousseau, D. M., S.B. Sitkin, R.S. Burt, and C. Camerer. 1998. "Not So Different After All: A Cross-Discipline View of Trust." *Academy of Management Review* 23, no. 3, pp. 393–404.

Schein, E.H., and P.A. Schein. 2021. *Humble Inquiry: The Gentle Art of Asking Instead of Telling*. Berrett-Koehler Publishers.

Schein, E.H. 1993. On dialogue, culture and organizational learning. *Organizational Dynamics* 22, no. 2, pp. 40–52

Schön, D.A. 2017. *The Reflective Practitioner: How Professionals Think in Action*. Routledge.

Schroeder, C. M., & Prentice, D. A. (1998). Exposing Pluralistic Ignorance to Reduce Alcohol Use Among College Students 1. *Journal of Applied Social Psychology*, 28(23), 2150–2180.

Shekshnia, S. 2018. "How to Be a Good Board Chair." *Harvard Business Review* 96, no. 2, pp. 96–105.

Shekshnia, S., and V. Zagieva. 2019. *Leading a Board*. Springer.

Sieber, T. 2019a. *Improving Board Dynamics and Open Dialogue: How Speaking Up Could Transform Corporate Boards* [Thesis]. Fontainebleau: INSEAD EMCCC.

Sieber, T. 2019b. "Mastering Corporate Startups—Opportunities and Challenges." In *Governance of Ventures*, ed. M. Hilb, 79–85. Haupt Verlag.

Sonnenfeld, J.A. 2002. "What Makes Great Boards Great?" *Harvard Business Review* 80, no. 9, pp. 106–113.

Sonnenfeld, J., M. Kusin, and E. Walton. 2013. "What CEOs Really Think of Their Boards." *Harvard Business Review* 91, no. 4, pp. 98–106.

Stanier, M.B. 2016. *The Coaching Habit: Say Less, Ask More & Change the Way You Lead Forever*. Box of Crayons Press.

State Street. January 2019. "Letter to the Board from Cyrus Taraporevala, President and CEO of State Street Global Advisors." Available from https://corpgov.law.harvard.edu/2019/01/15/2019-proxy-letter-aligning-corporate-culture-with-long-term-strategy/

Stein, S.J., and H.E. Book. 2011. *The EQ edge: Emotional Intelligence and Your Success*. John Wiley & Sons.

Stevenson, W.B., and R.F. Radin. 2015. "The Minds of the Board of Directors: The Effects of Formal Position and Informal Networks Among Board Members on Influence and Decision Making." *Journal of Management & Governance* 19, no. 2, pp. 421–460.

Sun, M. 2019. "More U.S. Companies Separating Chief Executive and Chairman Roles." *Wall Street Journal*. Available from www.wsj.com/articles/more-u-s-companies-separating-chief-executive-and-chairman-roles-11548288502

Thomann, C., and F. Schulz von Thun. 2003. *Klärungshilfe 1. Handbuch für Therapeuten, Gesprächshelfer und Moderatoren in schwierigen Gesprächen*. Reinbek: Rowohlt.

Vandewaerde, M., W. Voordeckers, F. Lambrechts, and Y. Bammens. 2011. "The Board of Directors as a Team: Getting Inside the Black Box." In *Proceedings of the 7th European Conference on Management, Leadership and Governance*, 436–442. Sophia-Antipolis, France.

Vuori, T.O., and Q.N. Huy. 2016. "Distributed Attention and shared Emotions in the Innovation Process: How Nokia Lost the Smartphone Battle." *Administrative Science Quarterly* 61, no. 1, pp. 9–51.

Zaleznik, A. 1997. "Real Work." *Harvard Business Review* 75, no. 6, pp. 53–59.

Zehnder, M. 2018. *The CEO: A Personal Reflection. Adapting to a Complex World*. Available from https://ceostudy.egonzehnder.com/The-CEO-report-EgonZehnder.pdf

About the Author

This book sits at the intersection of business experiences with boards and knowledge as a coach about the human behavior of leaders. **Dr. Thomas Sieber** combines these two fields of competence. As a long-term executive board member in charge of strategy and digital transformation, human resources, legal and compliance, and M&A, and a member of the board of directors, Chair, and secretary of the board of directors, he has vast and diverse practical experience with boards. With an Executive Master in Change at INSEAD where Thomas wrote about "improving board dynamics and open dialogue," his qualification as an ICF coach and commercial mediator, and practical board-coaching experience, he is perhaps uniquely placed to write about the human challenges at the top.

In 2020, Thomas Sieber was admitted as a research fellow at Harvard University with Professor Amy Edmondson as his academic sponsor, but COVID-19 restrictions prevented travel to the United States.

Having witnessed and experienced the rapidly evolving landscape of the corporate world from so many perspectives, boards, in particular, Thomas believes passionately that the dynamic of boards of directors and executive board teams requires a new way of operating: less of perfunctory governance and more heavily focused on creating effective team relationships and team responsibility.

Index

Lightning Source UK Ltd.
Milton Keynes UK
UKHW021018220422
401895UK00006B/162